AF881336

SMART MONEY, STRONG WOMEN

Your Complete Guide to Personal Finance, Wealth Building and Financial Freedom

Sarah Roughsedge

Design & Illustrated by Marianna Tofallis

Smart Money, Strong Women

Copyright © Sarah Roughsedge 2025
All rights reserved.

No part of this book may be reproduced in any form by photocopying or any electronic or mechanical means including information storage or retrieval systems, without permission in writing from both the copyright owner and publisher of the book.

ISBN: 978-1-8073-8040-3
Paperback

First published in 2025 by Eva Wealth Press, United Kingdom.
An environmentally friendly book printed and bound in England by bookvault, powered by printondemand-worldwide.

www.evawealth.co.uk

Design & Illustrated by Marianna Tofallis
Toffee Design Limited | www.toffee-design.com

Disclaimer:
This book is for general educational purposes only and does not constitute financial, legal, or tax advice. The information contained herein is based on sources believed to be reliable at the time of writing, but laws, regulations, and tax rules may change. Readers should obtain independent professional advice before making any financial decisions. Neither the author nor the publisher accepts responsibility for any loss or damage arising from reliance on this material.

For every woman who ever doubted her financial power.
May this book help you remember it was yours all along.
And to every client who has allowed me to help shape her journey and to those who have stood with me and shaped my own. Thank you.

Contents

"The most courageous act is still to think for yourself. Aloud." - Coco Chanel

Preface

"Whose secretary are you?"

I heard some version of that question at least a dozen times in my first year as a financial adviser. I was the only woman in the room, often the only person under 40, and apparently far too young and female to be taken seriously.

If this was how I was being treated within my profession as a qualified financial planner, what must it be like for other women trying to navigate this world as clients?

That question never left me and over the years, I watched a pattern emerge. Successful, intelligent women, doctors, business owners, executives, would sit across from me and say the same thing:

"I'm not very good with money."
"I don't really understand this stuff."
"I feel so stupid when it comes to investing."

These weren't stupid women. They were brilliant women who'd been conditioned from childhood to believe that money and investing wasn't for them. That it was a secret club with a membership only for men.

That's why I founded Eva Wealth Management for Women.

I brought together my background as a neuroscientist and my expertise as a Chartered Financial Planner to understand something the financial industry has long ignored: our relationship with money isn't just practical, it's deeply emotional.

As a mother of three, wife, and business owner, I know what it's like to try giving 100% to everything. Somewhere in that endless juggle, financial planning falls to the bottom. But when women understand their finances and take control of their money, something shifts. The 3am anxiety quiets. They sleep peacefully, knowing their family will be okay. They start saying yes to opportunities (even something as wild as learning to fly a plane, which in my case, solidified my journey in how to say yes to opportunities!). Money, when you understand it, isn't a burden. It's freedom.

This book represents what I've learned from working with hundreds of women. It combines practical financial wisdom with insights into the psychological patterns that shape our decisions. Whether you're a high-achieving professional, business owner, solopreneur, or navigating life changes, this is your companion on the journey to financial confidence.

Exclusion from financial conversations has cost women hugely. Not just years of worry and sleepless nights. But, missing out on wealth that's literally on the table and most devastatingly, missing out on living life to its absolute fullest.

This book is your roadmap to changing that. By the time you finish, you'll know which areas of your financial health need attention and which you can relax about. You'll have sources of help. And most importantly, you'll have what many women have been denied for too long: confidence. The confidence to ask questions without feeling stupid. To make decisions without second-guessing yourself. To know you're capable of creating the financial future you deserve.

You are absolutely capable of mastering your money. You always have been.

Welcome, it's time to build your wealth.

Sarah Roughsedge
Chartered Financial Planner

Introduction: Why This Book Is Different

If you've picked up this book, you're looking for something more than just another financial guide. Maybe you're successful in your career but feel uncertain about financial decisions, or you're going through a significant life change and need to take control of your financial future. Perhaps you simply want to feel more confident about money without being made to feel inadequate for what you don't yet know.

This book is different because it's written specifically for women, by a woman who understands both the science of money and the science of how we think about money. It acknowledges that women often approach money differently than men – not better or worse, just differently. And that's okay.

What you'll find in these pages isn't just financial theory.
Each chapter combines:

- clear, straightforward explanations of financial concepts
- real stories from women who've faced similar challenges
- practical steps you can take immediately
- the psychology behind money behaviours
- action points to build your confidence.

How to Use This Book

This book is designed to be both read and worked. At the end of each chapter, you'll find some short workbook exercises. They're the bridge between understanding and action. I encourage you to:

- Work through the book with a friend, partner, or trusted person. Money conversations become easier when shared.
- Leave all self-judgement at the door. Wherever you are financially, you're in the right place to begin.
- Complete the exercises as you go, or read through first and return to them. There's no wrong way to do this.

Most importantly, this book is part of a growing movement of women who refuse to be left behind financially. By reading this, you're joining that journey – you too become part of this rising collective.

Part 1: Foundation – Understanding Your Money Story

"Owning our story and loving ourselves through that process is the bravest thing we'll ever do." - Brené Brown

Every financial journey begins not with numbers, but with stories – the ones we've absorbed since childhood and the ones we continue to tell ourselves today. Part 1 of this book is about uncovering those patterns: how our upbringing, experiences, and beliefs shape our relationship with money. By exploring your money story, the gender dynamics that influence women's finances, and the roots of financial confidence, you'll start to see that the foundation of wealth is not just in your bank balance but in your mindset. This part sets the stage for everything that follows.

Chapter 1:
Your Relationship with Money – Understanding Your Money Mindset

Every woman has a money story. It's written in the way you feel when you check your bank balance, how you react to financial decisions, and what you believe about your ability to manage money. Understanding your money story is the first step toward making conscious choices about your financial future.

The Science of Money Stories

As a neuroscientist, I've observed how our brains create patterns and associations around money from an early age. These patterns become our money blueprint, influencing every financial decision we make. Research shows that by age seven, most of our basic money habits are formed. But here's the empowering truth: understanding these patterns gives us the power to choose which ones serve us and which ones we might want to adapt.

Our money stories aren't just about numbers – they're deeply intertwined with our emotions, memories, and experiences. When we make financial decisions, we're not just calculating returns or risks; we're responding to years of accumulated beliefs and patterns. And with that can come all sorts of behaviours that most of us won't even be consciously aware of, which either serve, or hinder us.

The Power of Your Money Story

Your money story is neither good nor bad – it's simply yours. Like a well-worn path through a garden, it represents the way you've learned to navigate your financial life. Some paths might lead exactly where you want to go, while others might take you on unnecessary detours. The key is understanding your path so you can choose whether to maintain it, modify it, or create new routes entirely. And that is one of the beautiful things about money stories; we may have allowed ours to define our path thus far (probably subconsciously, more often than not), but they do not have to define our future. We can reshape our future money mindset. Now that is super exciting!

Common Money Mindsets and Their Impact

Through my work, both as a chartered financial planner and a financial coach, I've observed various money mindsets that shape women's financial decisions. It's important to emphasise that whilst we can typically group various characteristics into several different categories or 'types', these aren't labels. We shouldn't take our money mindset category and see that as our definition. Rather these categories and descriptions highlight common patterns that can help us understand ourselves better. Once we have this understanding, we can become more aware and start to identify behaviours that can be sabotaging our progress. With identification and awareness then comes the ability to bring about change. Through the power of change we then witness transformation.

Your Money Mindset Type

I wanted this book to be a practical handbook for you. Empowering you to bring about transformation, not just a book of theory. You may already have some awareness of whether you feel you tend to spend money more easily than save it, or vice versa. But I would encourage you to go ahead and complete the following Money Mindset Quiz to help you identify both your primary and your secondary story mindset.

Quick Money Mindset Assessment

Discover Your Financial Personality in 5 Minutes

Instructions

Rate each statement on a scale of 1–5:

1 = Strongly Disagree, 2 = Somewhat Disagree, 3 = Neutral,

4 = Somewhat Agree, 5 = Strongly Agree

Your Money Attitudes & Behaviours	Rating (1–5)	
1. I prefer not to think about money matters and tend to postpone financial decisions.		
2. I regularly track my expenses and always ensure I have savings for emergencies.		
3. I find shopping or spending money gives me a sense of joy or relief.		
4. I'm concerned about how others perceive my financial status and lifestyle.		
5. I feel confident making financial decisions and enjoy learning about money management.		
6. I often leave financial statements unopened or bills unpaid until the last minute.		

Your Money Attitudes & Behaviours (continued)	Rating (1–5)	
7. I prioritise financial security over immediate enjoyment or purchases.		
8. I sometimes make impulse purchases that I later regret.		
9. My spending habits are influenced by what others might think of me.		
10. I have clear financial goals and regularly review my progress toward them.		
11. I feel anxious when I need to deal with money matters.		
12. I'm cautious with my money, sometimes to the point of missing out on experiences.		
13. I find it difficult to save for long-term goals because I prefer enjoying my money now.		
14. I sometimes spend to maintain appearances or to fit in with others.		
15. I'm comfortable discussing financial matters and seeking advice when needed.		

Scoring Guide
Calculate your total for each money type:

		Questions	Total
	Avoider Type	1, 6, 11	
	Guardian Type	2, 7, 12	
	Free Spirit Type	3, 8, 13	
	Status Seeker Type	4, 9, 14	
	Money Master Type	5, 10, 15	

Your highest score indicates your primary money type.
Your second-highest score indicates your secondary influence.

You will find lots of different names given to these different categories. I hope that the names I have chosen will make it easy to identify the characteristics that typically embody each common group and so help you in identifying your key money personality.

If your quiz results crowned you a Money Master, you may notice something missing in the examples that follow… you. And that's intentional. Not because you've done anything wrong – quite the opposite! The Money Master tends to have their systems, mindset and habits running so smoothly that there's very little for me to teach you in the story-based examples throughout the rest of the book. In fact, if anything, it might be that I need to take notes from you! So while you won't see yourself woven into the upcoming examples, take it as the compliment it is and a moment to consider whether your role might be to lead the way for others and assist them in their onward journey.

PAUSE HERE: Did one type sound uncomfortably familiar? Jot down the sentence or belief that stood out most to you.

The Status Seeker

Does This Sound Like You?

- Your net worth feels like a measure of self-worth
- Money is a powerful symbol of success and status
- You pursue financial achievements with passionate intensity
- our purchases tell a story of ambition and potential
- External validation drives your financial choices

Typical Status Seeker Characteristics:

- Tendency to spend freely on status-enhancing items
- Potential for accumulating debt in pursuit of image
- Seeing expensive purchases as personal statements
- Linking personal value to financial achievements
- Prioritising appearances over long-term financial stability

Positive Aspects: Ambitious drive, success-oriented, achievement-focused, strong motivation for wealth building.

Challenges: May overspend on status items, potential for debt accumulation in pursuit of image.

Common Belief: "My success is measured by what I can afford"

The Guardian

Does This Sound Like You?

- Money is your security blanket
- Banks are your best friends
- "Good enough" is your shopping motto
- Bargain hunting is your superpower
- Financial safety is your top priority

Typical Guardian Characteristics:

- Difficulty spending money on yourself
- Expert at finding sales and discounts
- Uncomfortable admitting to full-price purchases
- Always preparing for the hypothetical "rainy day"
- Persistent anxiety about potential financial disasters
- Sees money as a protective shield against uncertainty

Positive Aspects: Excellent at saving, security-focused, risk-aware, thorough research skills.

Challenges: May be overcautious with investments, difficulty spending on personal enjoyment.

Common Belief: "Better safe than sorry"

The Free Spirit

Does This Sound Like You?

- Money flows through your hands like water
- Shopping brings you joy and a sense of excitement
- Possessions feel like extensions of your personal identity
- Generosity is your middle name – both to yourself and others

Typical Free Spirit Characteristics:

- Closets filled with unused items, tags still attached
- Frequent packages and shopping bags
- Tendency to wow friends with gifts
- Hidden purchase spots in your home
- Masterful at self-convincing phrases like "I deserve this"
- Potential challenges with impulse buying and debt avoidance

Positive Aspects: Generous, enthusiastic about life, values experiences, quick to embrace opportunities.

Challenges: Impulse buying tendencies, potential for debt accumulation, difficulty with strict budgets.

Common Belief: "Money is meant to be enjoyed"

The Avoider

Does This Sound Like You?

- Financial conversations make you uncomfortable
- Bills create a sense of overwhelming dread
- Money feels like a complex puzzle you'd rather ignore
- Financial decisions feel paralyzing
- You hope someone else will handle the money matters

Typical Avoider Characteristics:

- Tendency to hide purchases from partners
- Accumulating unopened bills
- Delegating financial decisions to others
- Experiencing anxiety around money discussions
- Creating elaborate avoidance strategies
- Feeling stuck in a cycle of financial uncertainty

Positive Aspects: Often highly capable in other areas, strong desire for simplicity, awareness of need for change.

Challenges: May accumulate unopened bills, tendency to delegate all financial decisions, financial anxiety.

Common Belief: "I'm just not good with money"

Working With Your Money Mindset Archetype

Understanding your archetype isn't about being boxed into a category, it's about recognising patterns so you can work with them more effectively. Each archetype has unique strengths to leverage and specific challenges to be aware of.

For Status Seekers: Channel your achievement drive into building real wealth, not just the appearance of wealth. Set goals for net worth growth rather than lifestyle inflation. Your ambition is a superpower when directed toward genuine wealth building.

For Guardians: Your saving discipline is a superpower. The challenge is learning when and how to deploy those savings strategically for growth and enjoyment. Your careful nature makes you excellent at research and due diligence.

For Free Spirits: Your openness to experiences can be an asset in investing. Create systems that automate your savings so you can spend guilt-free on what matters to you. Your generosity and enthusiasm are strengths when channelled intentionally.

For Avoiders: Start small and build systems that require minimal daily decisions. Your goal is to create financial autopilot so money management becomes effortless. Your awareness of the need for change is already a significant first step.

Important Note: Please keep in mind that money mindsets exist on a spectrum, and there are often shades of grey. For example, you may identify primarily as a Guardian but also recognise traits of an Avoider in your relationship with money. This is perfectly normal! If you find yourself reflecting aspects of multiple mindsets, feel free to embrace the insights from both and apply them to your financial journey. Understanding these nuances allows you to adopt a more balanced and effective approach, blending strategies from different money personalities to create an approach that works best for you.

Understanding Your Personal Story

Whilst we may all broadly fall within 1 or 2 money mindset personalities, your money story is unique to you. It is shaped by:

- family influences
- cultural background
- life experiences
- professional journey
- personal values.

It is incredible to think that our money habits are already wired into us by the age of 7. A great way of considering this is through the following exercise. Close your eyes for a moment and allow your memory to wander as far back as you can. Now tune into your first money memory. Was it your parents talking (or not talking) about money? Was it being given pocket money? Was it feeling embarrassed because your parents didn't have enough money to buy you new clothes to fit you? Was it finding a coin on the floor somewhere? Was it being given money for an ice cream on holiday?

Each of us has our own collection of memories about money that have interlinked themselves upon each previous memory. As we weave our experiences together, we form a natural bias to seek out, or perceive, the same interpretations from each experience. It's simply the way our brains work. There's a reassurance, or a safety, that our brains take from a repeating message – even if we don't like the message.

QUICK CHECK-IN: What's the very first money memory that just popped into your head? Write down a few words now before it slips away.

How Your Money Story Affects Every Financial Decision

Now that you understand your archetype, you'll start noticing how it influences every aspect of your financial life:

Investment Decisions: Status Seekers might gravitate toward "impressive" investments, while Guardians prefer safe options, Free Spirits enjoy socially responsible funds, and Avoiders might avoid investing altogether.

Spending Patterns: Each archetype has different spending triggers and comfort zones. Understanding yours helps you make conscious choices rather than automatic reactions.

Financial Goals: Your archetype influences what financial freedom looks like to you. Status Seekers might aim for visible wealth, Guardians for security, Free Spirits for flexibility, and Avoiders for simplicity.

Money Conversations: How you talk about money with partners, family, and advisors is shaped by your archetype. Recognising this helps improve these crucial conversations.

The beautiful thing about understanding your money story is that awareness creates choice. You're no longer running unconscious patterns, you're making deliberate decisions about which aspects of your archetype serve you and which you might want to evolve.

The Impact on Decision-Making

Our money stories influence decisions in ways we might not realise. Here are some examples which you might recognise:

Daily Financial Habits

- Spending patterns: whether you feel comfortable treating yourself or experience guilt after purchases; if you're drawn to bargains even when you don't need them; or whether you avoid looking at your bank balance to sidestep uncomfortable feelings about money.
- Saving behaviours: your default approach to any extra money that comes in; do you immediately save it, spend it, or feel anxious if you're not building a cushion? Some people hoard money out of fear, while others struggle to save because spending feels like the only way to enjoy life now.
- Budget management: whether you track every penny meticulously, avoid budgets entirely because they feel restrictive, or find yourself constantly justifying exceptions to your own rules. Your comfort level with structure around money often reflects deeper beliefs about control and security.

Investment Choices

- How risk is perceived: what feels like "dangerous risk" versus "smart opportunity" is deeply personal and often rooted in past experiences. Someone who grew up in financial instability might see any investment as gambling, while someone raised with financial confidence might view not investing as the real risk.
- What feels like a "safe" option: your definition of safety might mean keeping cash where you can see it, investing in property because it's tangible, or trusting index funds because they feel less speculative. These preferences often reflect what you witnessed or were taught about money growing up.
- When to take action versus wait: whether you act quickly on opportunities or need extensive research and reassurance before making a move; if market dips make you panic-sell or see a buying opportunity; or whether you procrastinate on financial decisions altogether because they trigger anxiety or overwhelm.

Long-term Planning

- Retirement vision: not just the practical numbers, but what retirement represents to you emotionally; freedom, fear of irrelevance, reward for hard work, or something you can't quite imagine because you've never seen it modelled in a way that feels attainable or desirable.
- Legacy goals: whether leaving money behind feels important or unnecessary; if you want to support your children financially or believe they should be entirely self-sufficient; and how you balance taking care of future generations with enjoying your wealth now.
- Life priorities: what you're willing to sacrifice financially and what you're not; whether experiences matter more than possessions, security trumps adventure, or whether you're caught between competing values that make financial decisions feel like impossible trade-offs.

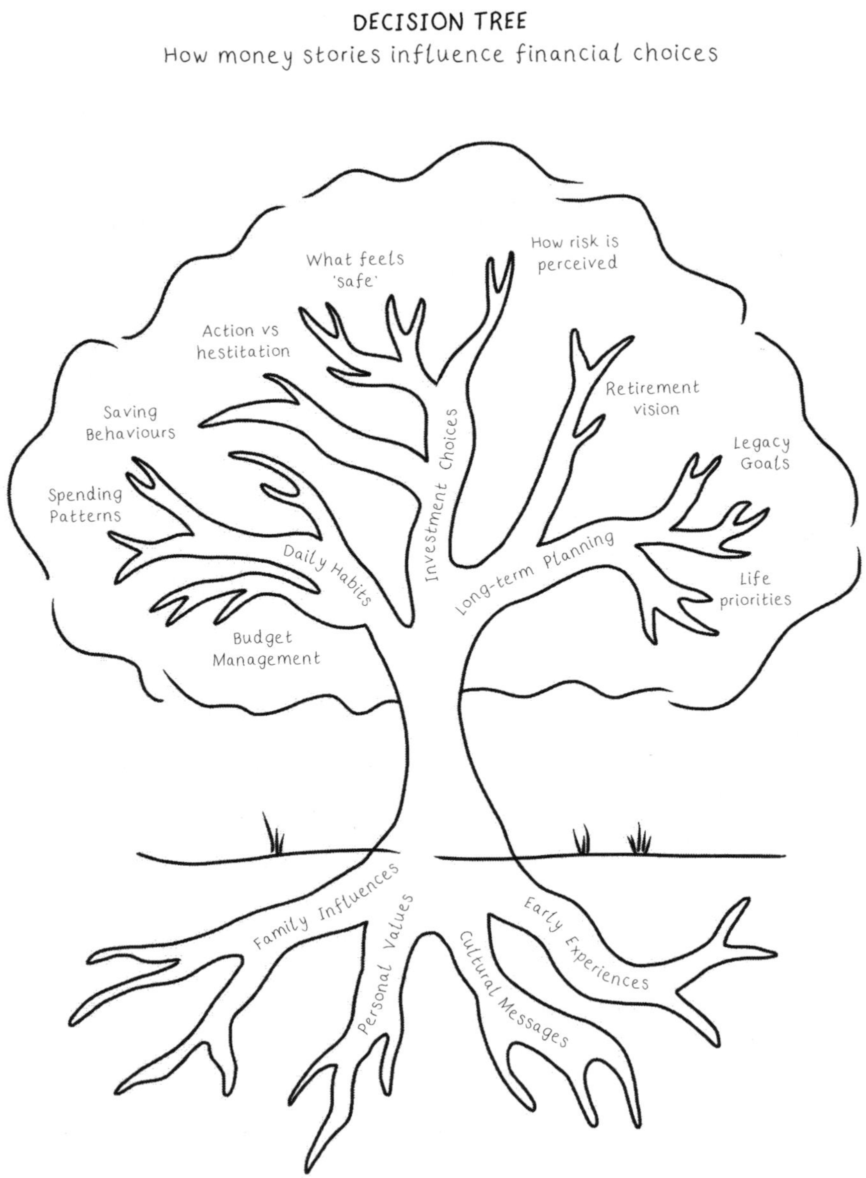
DECISION TREE
How money stories influence financial choices
What feels 'safe'
How risk is perceived
Action vs hestitation
Retirement vision
Saving Behaviours
Legacy Goals
Investment Choices
Spending Patterns
Long-term Planning
Daily Habits
Life priorities
Budget Management
Family Influences
Personal Values
Early Experiences
Cultural Messages

Recognising Patterns in Action

I want you to think about the following examples:

- Hesitating to invest despite having adequate savings: you have money sitting in a low-interest savings account, and logically you know you could be growing it, but something holds you back. Perhaps you're waiting for the "perfect" moment, or the idea of moving that money into investments triggers a sense of vulnerability or fear of loss. This hesitation often stems from beliefs about security – that cash in hand is the only true safety, or that investing is for "other people" who understand money better. You might find yourself endlessly researching without ever taking action, or creating reasons why "now isn't the right time."
- Always choosing the safest option, even when young enough to take calculated risks: you have decades until retirement, but your portfolio looks like someone nearing their final working years. Every investment decision tilts toward preservation rather than growth. This pattern might reflect a deep-seated belief that losing money (even temporarily) would be catastrophic, perhaps because you witnessed financial loss growing up or were taught that risk-taking with money is reckless. While caution has its place, playing it too safe when you have time on your side can mean missing opportunities for your money to work harder for you.
- Putting everyone else's financial needs first: your children's wishes, your parents' expectations, your partner's dreams – everyone's financial priorities seem to come before your own. You might justify this as being generous or responsible, but underneath there's often a belief that your needs don't matter as much, or that taking care of yourself financially is somehow selfish. This can show up as funding adult children's lifestyles while neglecting your own retirement, saying yes to loans you can't afford, or feeling guilty about spending money on yourself even when you have it to spare.
- Avoiding financial discussions or decisions: bills pile up unopened, you change the subject when friends talk about money, or you defer all financial decisions to someone else. This avoidance isn't laziness, it's often rooted in anxiety, shame, or feeling overwhelmed. Perhaps money conversations in your family were linked to conflict, or you absorbed the message that talking about money is impolite or shameful. Maybe you fear discovering you're "behind" where you should be, so not looking feels safer than facing reality. The problem is that avoidance doesn't make financial challenges disappear; it usually makes them grow.

These aren't character flaws, they are simply patterns that may or may not serve your current goals. Every one of these behaviours made sense at some point, perhaps as a response to what you witnessed, experienced, or were taught. The question isn't whether you're doing something "wrong," but whether these patterns are helping you build the financial future you actually want, or whether they're holding you back from it.

The Growth Opportunity

The beauty of understanding your money story is that it opens doors to self-awareness. This isn't just about noticing what behaviours and decisions you might be making as a result of your money story, but importantly, its recognising your patterns without judgement. Many of us have become expert self-judgers! We are "just not very good at this", or are "so stupid". These are self-judgements I have heard over and over again from the women I have worked with. So, I hope that you did exactly as I asked at the start of this book – you left all your self-judgement and criticisms outside the door and you have chosen to embrace this time for the opportunity for growth and empowerment!

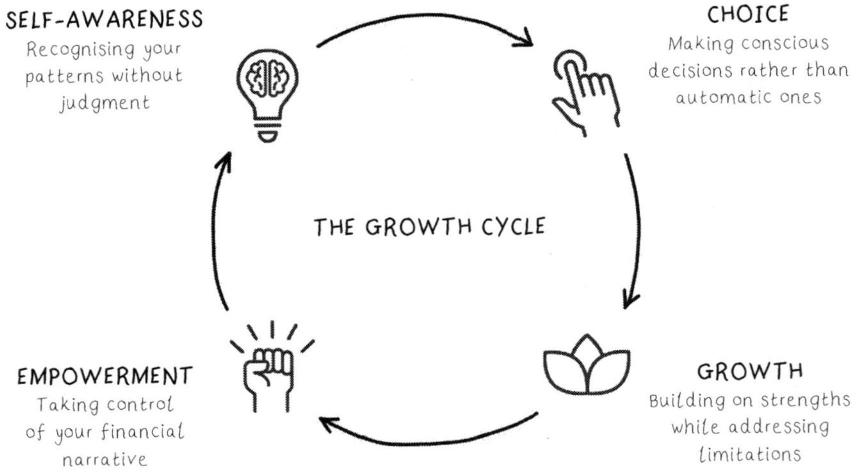

Remember, more often than not it is a conscious choice first, before the feeling comes after.

The Neuroscience of Growth

You might be wondering why I'm making such a big deal about noticing your patterns without judgement. Well, here's the fascinating bit: your brain is wired in such a way that this simple act is what unlocks change.

Most of our financial habits live in the basal ganglia. This is the part of the brain that runs on autopilot. It's like your brain's habit manager, storing the "scripts" you picked up about money years ago. That's why you might find yourself overspending, avoiding decisions, or endlessly saving without ever consciously choosing to; your brain is simply running its old programme.

Now, when you judge yourself ("I'm terrible with money," "I'm so stupid"), your amygdala, the brain's threat detector, lights up. This triggers your stress response, releasing cortisol and narrowing your ability to think clearly. In that moment, you're not in growth mode, you're in survival mode.

But here's the good news: when you step back and simply notice a pattern with curiosity instead of criticism, you switch on your prefrontal cortex, the rational, reflective part of your brain. This creates what neuroscientists call a prediction error: your brain was expecting shame, but you gave it compassion instead. And that tiny shift is what opens the door to neuroplasticity, the brain's ability to rewire itself.

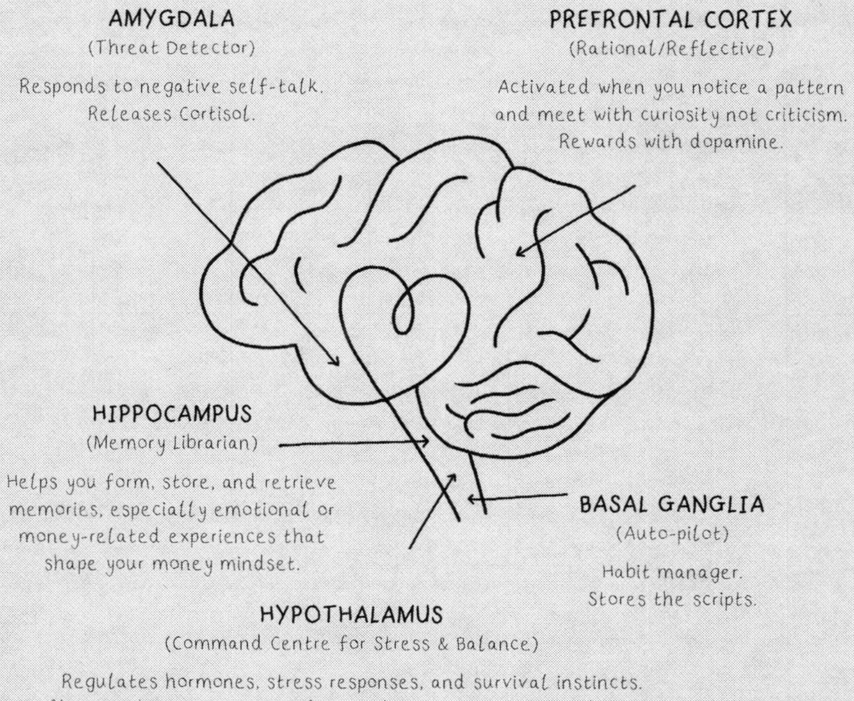

Every time you then make a conscious choice to do something different, you're laying down a new neural pathway. And when you repeat that choice, your brain rewards you with a hit of dopamine (your feel-good chemical), which encourages you to keep going. Over time, those new pathways get stronger and stronger, while the old ones fade.

This is why growth doesn't come from perfection, but from practice. Step by step, your brain literally reshapes itself so that new, empowering behaviours start to feel more natural and automatic. That's when empowerment happens: when you're no longer trapped by the old scripts, but free to write your own money story.

Now that we understand a little more about Money Stories and why, even when some of us may feel shame, there is none, I have created an opportunity for you to unpack your money story further so you can better understand how your story has formed over the years and how this is potentially influencing your decisions today. There will be both helpful and unhelpful behaviours that have formed.

Understanding your money story is just the beginning in this journey of financial empowerment. My hope is that you have had some "aha" and "hmm, that makes so much sense" moments as you have worked through this first chapter. Remember, theory is just that until you put it into action. Each one of us is a hugely complex mix of experiences, teachings, feelings and emotions. Oh, and let's not forget the ticking time bomb that are our hormones too. Let's identify what has gotten us to where we are today and what is within our control through these exercises to take us beyond where we thought we could get to and re-write our money story to create the future we want.

In the next chapter, we'll explore how gender-specific experiences shape our financial journey and why women need a unique approach to financial planning.

Chapter 1 Workbook Exercises: Understanding Your Money Story

1. **Quick Knowledge Check:**
   Which money story type resonates most with you?
   ☐ The Guardian ☐ The Free Spirit ☐ The Status Seeker ☐ Avoider

2. **One Key Reflection: Complete this sentence:**
   "My biggest money pattern that might be holding me back is..."

3. **Priority Action This Week:** Choose one:
   - ☐ Track my spending for 7 days to identify patterns
   - ☐ Have an honest conversation about money with someone I trust
   - ☐ Write down my earliest money memory and what it taught me

4. **Sign up to MyWealthVault** from Eva Wealth and explore your money personality in more detail!

Chapter 2:
The Gender Money Gap – Why Women Need a Different Approach

Claire, a brilliant surgeon in her mid-forties, had spent years building her career while raising three children. Despite her impressive income, she felt behind in her financial journey compared to her male colleagues. "I took three career breaks for my children," she explained, "and now I'm wondering if I'll ever catch up." Claire's story isn't unique – it's a pattern I've seen repeatedly and it perfectly illustrates why women need a different approach to financial planning.

Understanding the Gap

The gender money gap isn't just about headlines announcing pay differences – though those certainly matter. It's about understanding the unique financial journey women navigate throughout their lives. Think of it like planning a road trip: while everyone might be heading to the same destination (of financial security), women often face different terrain, unexpected detours, and unique challenges along the way.

THE GAP TIMELINE

Timeline showing key life events and their financial impact, for typical female financial journeys

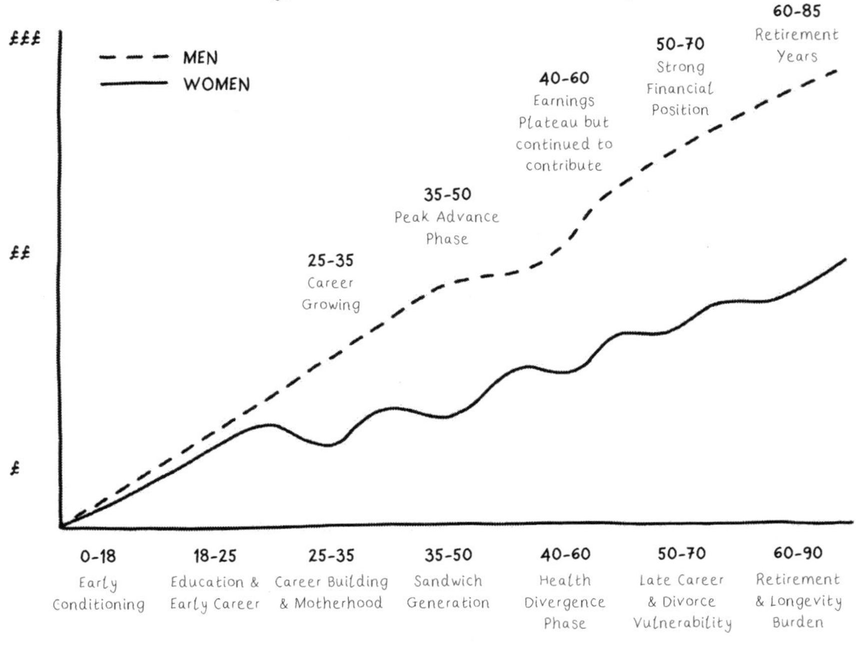

Career Patterns

Let's talk about career breaks first. Whether it's for childcare, caring for elderly parents, or other family responsibilities, women are more likely to step away from their careers temporarily. Taking just a two-year career break to care for young children and elderly parents won't just cost you two years of salary – it impacts on pension contributions, career progression, and your investment timeline.

But here's what's fascinating: many women develop incredible financial skills during these periods. Managing a household budget during reduced income, making strategic decisions about childcare costs versus career opportunities, and efficiently allocating limited resources – these are all valuable financial management skills that often go unrecognised. Yet they look different from the more traditionally thought of financial skills such as "investing". This does not mean women are financially less capable than men at all. It's just that as a society, we have placed a higher order of perceived importance or skill with finances on areas such as investing, rather than running a tight household budget.

Consider these common scenarios:

- Part-time work phases often coincide with peak earning years, resulting in lower overall earnings amongst women who have chosen to reduce their working hours to either have children or care for family members
- Women's careers often accelerate later in life, meaning greater financial resources become available, just when traditional financial advice suggests reducing risk
- Negotiation experiences differ significantly, with women often facing different social expectations and responses.

Any of these scenarios alone are likely to create a differential in lifetime earnings amongst women compared to men. When you combine several of these together, its not hard to see that women's lifetime earnings can be hard hit compared to men's, just from these wider family choices.

Life Expectancy

It's now a widely recognised fact that on average, women live 3–5 years longer than men. This isn't just a biological curiosity – it has profound implications for financial planning. Let's think about it in terms of the traditional relationship, which still forms the majority of formal partnerships. The male partner may be 3 years older than the female partner. The female partner will then on average live 3–5 years longer than her partner. So she could be living 6–8 years alone after losing her partner and possibly financially independent for the first time in over 60 years. It is a fact; as women we need our money to last longer, we're more likely to handle finances alone in later life, and we face higher lifetime healthcare costs.

Barbara, a widow in her seventies, found herself managing finances for the first time after 45 years of marriage. "I wish I'd been more involved earlier," she told me. "I'm not just learning about money – I'm learning about myself." Barbara's story inspired me to ensure all my clients, regardless of their relationship status, develop financial confidence early.

Societal Influences

We're all continuously influenced by media and others around us. So, over time, the messages we receive about money through media channels and wider society will have formed a key part in the assumptions we have made. These messages have often differed dramatically based on gender. From childhood piggy banks to retirement planning, the narrative around women and money has historically focused more on saving and budgeting than investing and wealth creation. Just a simple Google search for money adverts over different time periods highlights how polarised the messaging has been for men and women over the years.

The following diagram shows the evolution of gender-differentiated messaging around money over time.

THE EVOLUTION OF GENDERED MONEY MESSAGING

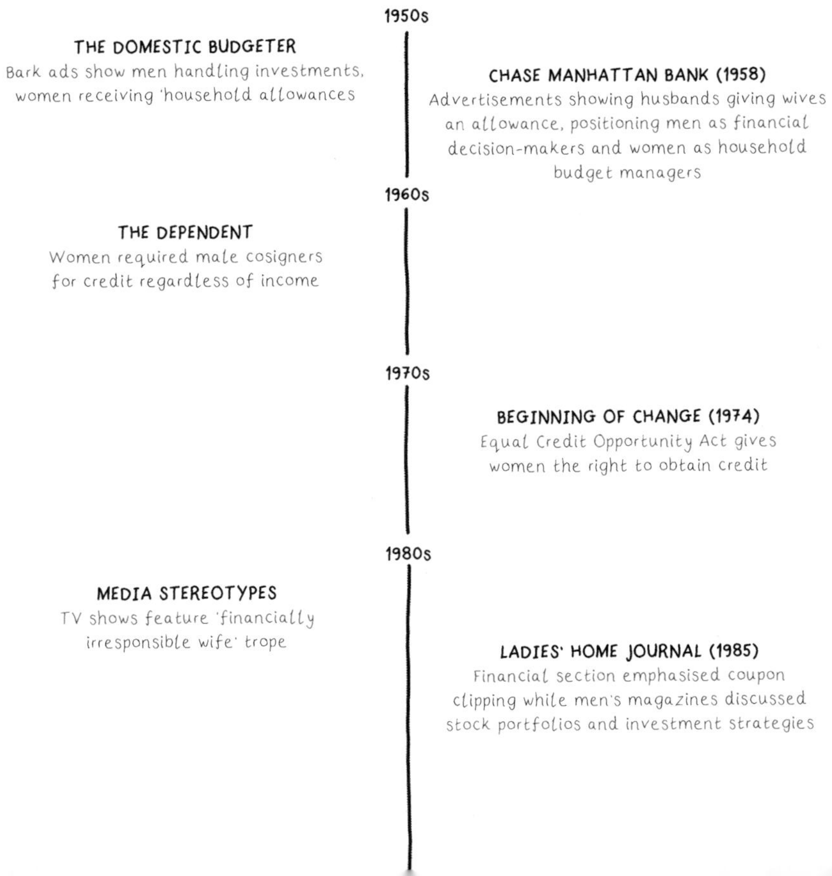

1990s

CONSUMER VS. INVESTOR
Mutual funds for women emphasise security not growth

2000s

PINK BRANDING
Financial apps use pink with focus on saving not investing

CITIBANK'S 'WOMEN & CO' (2000)
Used softer colours and emphasised protecting assets rather than growing them - different from general market materials focused on wealth building

2010s

THE FIN-FLUENCER
Rise of the Financial influencers and social media communities

2020s

EMPOWERMENT SHIFT
Campaigns address the gender investment gap and wealth creation

PRUDENTIALS 'OWN YOUR FUTURE' (2020)
A positive shift - specifically address historical messaging by encouraging women to take control of their financial future through investing, not just saving

Here's why this has such a significant impact. Let's assume David and Sally, twins, have grown up to the age of 60 and are considering their future retirement years. David, tuning in to the investing and wealth creation messages from society has done just that – has learnt that magic lesson which can appear written in code just for men, on how to invest – and has amassed an investment of £250,059 from investing £250 per month over the last 20 years.

Sally, tuning in to the saving and budgeting messages from society has run a superb family budget and managed the family finances through all the financial pressures they have faced over the years, and still managed to put aside £250 per month. Sally saved hard in her bank's savings accounts and now has a pot of money worth £136,975.

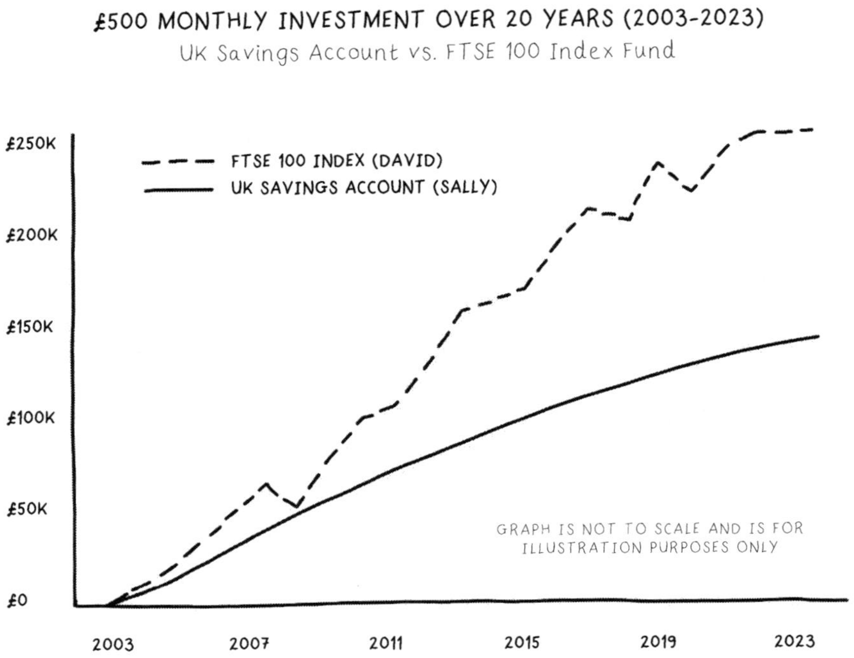

The visual tells the story starkly: two lines on a graph, starting at the same point twenty years ago. David's investment line, although a bumpy one, rises upward, ending at £250,059. Sally's savings line, whilst steady, never comes close to finishing at the same amassed wealth as David, ending at £136,975. Same monthly contribution. Same family. Different messages. Different outcomes. A gap of over £113,000 – not from lack of effort or intelligence, but from the societal narratives each absorbed about what they were 'supposed' to do with money.

This really stood out to me when I received a phone call one day from a young lady enquiring as to my services. She was fresh out of university, just a few months into her first job. Her words still ring loud and clear in my head "I just don't want to get left behind. I want to start off on the same footing as my male peers. Somehow, they just seem to be privy to a whole other language and source of knowledge about money and investing that girls aren't".

At that stage I had my traditional financial planning service for women with significant assets to invest. I was ahead of the curve offering this, whilst many firms still did not recognise that many women needed a different approach. But I wasn't yet in a position to be able to offer a service for women at the start of their financial journey, built around education and empowerment. But from that moment, it sparked in me a burning desire to develop something for all women (and I am thrilled to invite you to visit **mywealthvault.co.uk** to find out more if you are interested!).

The Real Impact

When we look at how these factors compound over time, the numbers tell a compelling story:

- The average woman's pension pot at retirement is typically 40% smaller than a man's.
- Women's investment confidence often lags behind their actual financial capability.
- Long-term wealth accumulation can be significantly impacted by career breaks and part-time work.
- Women typically need to save a higher percentage of their income to achieve the same retirement lifestyle as men, due to longer life expectancy.

Isn't that staggering? The culmination of these different factors paint a powerful picture of why the financial gender gap exists. But whilst it is helpful to understand why this gap exists, here's the crucial point: now we understand this and with the help of this book, you can start to plan accordingly.

Turning Challenges into Opportunities

This is where we get to change the narrative moving forward. Every challenge I've mentioned also presents an opportunity for strategic planning and innovative solutions. I'm not suggesting that all will be straightforward or easy now that we understand why there is a gender disparity. But by being aware and bringing these topics into our conversations at home and at work, we can plan with more awareness.

Let me share some examples:

Career Breaks

Instead of viewing career breaks as purely negative, we can plan for them proactively. I often find that there is a different emotional approach to this amongst couples who are planning for a career break to travel or take a sabbatical, compared to those who are planning time off for a family, which in itself is a fascinating observation. This raises 2 key points; the opportunity for a wider discussion around financial expectations as a couple (how do you view your financial contributions to the family household, how do you view your time and energy contribution, how do you view your parenting responsibilities), and also then the ability to plan for this season.

I have worked with clients in this season of life to better prepare for this time through:

- Creating a "career break fund" separate from her emergency savings
- Creating a plan to maintain her professional certifications during her break
- Keeping her pension contributions going through careful budgeting (this is often one of the first outgoings I see stopped and the knock on effect of this for retirement planning can be huge)
- Structuring her investments to compensate for the contribution gap

A Note For Couples

If you are in a long term relationship, there is an added dimension compared to a woman living and operating alone. Whilst initially it may appear that the financial implications of career breaks may be less daunting than for an individual contemplating this, there is the added complexity of communication and expectation to work through.

Every couple will have their way of running their household finances. Some couples will operate their finances entirely separately and each pay a contribution towards the household costs. Sometimes this contribution is split equally and sometimes it is proportioned according to each partner's earnings. Others pool everything. Whilst others pool everything and then allocate a spending fund each for personal spending. And so on. There is no right or wrong way and it is for each couple of work out what approach works best for them. However you run your household finances, ensuring that you communicate openly and regularly will help you face into these decisions more effectively.

The Financial Date Night: Your Communication Tool

Regular money conversations don't have to feel heavy. Try framing them as Financial Date Nights – a structured yet comfortable way to stay aligned on your shared financial journey.

Setting the Scene: Choose a calm space, pour a glass of wine, eliminate distractions, and set a 60–90 minute time limit. Commit to curiosity over criticism.

The Golden Rules:

- Listen without interrupting
- Use "I" statements about feelings and concerns
- Take breaks if emotions run high
- End with appreciation for engaging together

Your Quarterly Agenda:

- Celebrate Wins *(5 min)*
  What's gone well financially since your last chat?
- Review Spending *(15 min)*
  Are you on track with your budget and goals?
- Address Concerns *(20 min)*
  What's causing stress or needs discussion?
- Plan Ahead *(15 min)*
  Upcoming expenses, life changes, or big decisions?
- Adjust Your System *(5 min)*
  Does your financial structure still work for both of you?

Important Topics to Rotate Through:

- How contributions will adjust during career breaks or income changes
- Pension planning and who's contributing what
- Protection (life insurance, wills, beneficiaries)
- Individual spending freedom vs shared expenses
- Career development and earning potential
- Major purchases or life transitions

Making It Work for Your Relationship: Whether you operate fully joint, fully separate, or somewhere in between, what matters is that both partners feel heard, respected, and clear on expectations – especially when life changes like career breaks are on the horizon.

The Bottom Line: These conversations aren't about achieving perfection or eliminating disagreement. They're about building understanding and staying connected to your shared goals, even when individual circumstances shift.

1. Investment Strategy

With typically longer life spans, women actually have the advantage of more time for investments to grow. This isn't just a demographic curiosity, it's a potential financial advantage that's rarely discussed in traditional financial planning. This can translate into:

- greater ability to recover from market downturns
- more time for compound interest to work its magic
- opportunities for slightly higher risk tolerance in appropriate circumstances
- better long-term returns when invested strategically.

When I explain this to my clients, many are surprised. After all, we typically hear about longevity as a financial challenge, not an opportunity. But think about this: the average woman in the UK lives about 3–5 years longer than the average man. Those extra years create several investing advantages that can translate into:

2. Greater ability to recover from market downturns

With a longer investment horizon, temporary market volatility associated with investing becomes less threatening. I've worked with many women who initially feared market fluctuations, but when we mapped out their likely 25-30+ year retirement timeline, they realised they had multiple market cycles ahead to recover from any downturns.

Take Rebecca, a client who was nearing retirement during the 2020 market crash. While many of her peers panic-sold, we reviewed her longer time horizon and stayed invested. The markets recovered, and she benefited fully from the subsequent growth, an opportunity she might have missed with a shorter perspective.

3. More time for compound interest to work its magic

Compound interest has been called the eighth wonder of the world, and for good reason. What many don't realise is how dramatically compounding accelerates in later years.

For example, if you invest £10,000 at a 7% average annual return, after 20 years you'd have about £38,700. But after 30 years, just 10 more years, that same initial investment would grow to over £76,100. Those extra years that women often have can nearly double the results without contributing an additional pound.

4. Opportunities for slightly higher risk tolerance in appropriate circumstances

Traditional advice often suggests becoming extremely conservative with investments as you age. While reducing risk is important, women's longer horizons may allow for maintaining a more balanced approach.

For instance, at 65, a woman might still have a 25–30 year investment horizon, similar to a 35–40 year old man in terms of remaining lifespan. This doesn't mean taking inappropriate risks, but it might mean keeping a meaningful portion of investments in growth assets rather than shifting entirely to income-focused investments.

5. Better long-term returns when invested strategically
With more time, women can often benefit from:

- More strategic asset allocation across different time horizons
- Greater total return from reinvested dividends over additional years
- Higher probability of capturing multiple economic growth cycles
- More time to benefit from pound-cost averaging strategies

The key insight is that women's financial plans should reflect their actual life expectancy, not generic models that might underestimate their timeline by 5–10 years. This perspective shift alone can transform how we approach investment strategy and potentially improve long-term financial outcomes.

Childcare Cost Analysis: Career Break Planning

The statistics we've explored paint a clear picture of the financial challenges women face, but nowhere is this more complex than in the decisions around career breaks for childcare. This isn't simply about weighing nursery fees against your salary, it's about understanding the true, long-term cost of career interruptions and making informed decisions based on complete information, not just immediate cash flow.

Every year, thousands of highly capable women make career decisions based on incomplete financial analysis. They calculate the cost of childcare against their current take-home pay and conclude it's not worth working. But this calculation misses the bigger picture: career progression, pension contributions, skills maintenance, and future earning potential. Let's examine the real numbers.

The True Cost Calculation

Childcare costs extend beyond the monthly nursery fee and its important to consider not only the obvious financial costs, but also the hidden costs from which the impact is only seen later on.

Direct Costs (Annual):

- Nursery fees: £1,200–£2,000/month per child
- Holiday care: Additional £2,000–£4,000
- Sick child care: £500–£1,500
- Transport/logistics: £600–£1,200

Hidden Costs:

- Career progression delay: £50,000–£150,000 lifetime impact
- Pension contributions gap: £30,000–£80,000 at retirement
- Reduced professional network development
- Skills depreciation in fast-moving fields

Decision Framework: Work vs. Stay Home

The Break-Even Analysis

Formula: Net salary after tax/NI – (Childcare costs + Work expenses + Career impact) = True financial position

Example – Marketing Manager (£35k salary):

Take-home pay – £28,200: this is what actually lands in your account after income tax and National Insurance contributions, not the headline salary figure.

Childcare (2 children) – £20,400: full-time nursery for two children at £850 per month each, or £10,200 annually per child. This figure can vary dramatically by region – London and the South East often see costs 20-30% higher, while some areas have slightly lower rates. This doesn't include the inevitable extras: settling-in fees, late pickup charges, holiday clubs, or the weeks you still pay for when your child is ill or the nursery is closed.

Work expenses (travel, clothes, lunches) – £2,400: the hidden costs of working: £100 monthly on commuting (petrol, parking, or train fares), maintaining a professional wardrobe, grabbing lunch because you didn't have time to prepare it, and the occasional emergency taxi when childcare arrangements fall through. These "small" expenses add up to £200 per month, or £2,400 annually.

Net financial benefit of working – £5,400: on paper, you're earning £5,400 more by working than staying home. That's £450 per month, not nothing, but hardly the full £35,000 salary you started with. When you break it down, you're effectively working full-time for £2.77 per hour after childcare and expenses.

But consider:

Career progression lost – £5,000–£10,000 annually in future earnings: taking a career break doesn't just freeze your salary, it often means missing promotions, pay rises, and skill development that your peers continue to accumulate. If you were on track for a promotion from £35,000 to £40,000 within two years, stepping away could mean re-entering at the same or even a lower level. Over a decade, this compounds significantly. The "motherhood penalty" is well-documented: women who take extended breaks earn 2–4% less per year out of work when they return.

Pension gap – £2,800 annually: your employer likely contributes around 5–8% of your salary to your pension (in this case, approximately £2,800 annually). When you stop working, these contributions stop. Over a five-year break, that's £14,000 in lost pension contributions, which would have grown with compound interest over the following decades. This pension gap is one of the key reasons women retire with significantly smaller pots than men.

True cost of leaving – £7,800–£12,800 annually: when you factor in lost career progression and pension contributions, stepping away from work costs you substantially more than the £5,400 net benefit you calculated. The true annual cost is between £7,800 and £12,800 and this doesn't account for intangible losses like professional confidence, network connections, or skills currency.

Alternative Strategies

Rather than the binary choice of full-time work or complete career break, you could consider these options:

Flexible Working Negotiation – 4-day week, compressed hours, job sharing: many employers are more open to flexible arrangements than people assume, especially if you propose a clear plan. A 4-day week might reduce your salary by 20% (to £28,000), but childcare costs could drop by 20–40% depending on the arrangement, making your net position similar or better. Compressed hours (full-time hours over 4 days) maintain your salary while reducing a day of childcare. Job sharing allows you to retain a meaningful role while working part-time. The key is approaching this as a professional proposal, not a personal favour. Frame it around business benefits like retention, productivity, and continuity.

Career Pivot Timing – Use break for strategic upskilling/career change: if you're considering a career break anyway, use it strategically. Is there a qualification that would open higher-paying opportunities? Could you retrain into a more flexible or better-paid field? Rather than seeing the break as "lost time," structure it as an investment period. For example, qualifying as an accountant, project manager, or tech professional during a 1–2 year break could increase your earning potential by 30–50% upon return.

Gradual Return – Phased return over 6–12 months: rather than going from full-time parent to full-time employee overnight (which often leads to burnout and resignations), negotiate a phased return. Start with 2–3 days per week for the first few months, increasing gradually. This allows your child to adjust to childcare, lets you rebuild your professional stamina, and gives you time to establish reliable routines. Many parents find this transition far more sustainable.

Freelance/Consulting – Maintain skills and network while caring: even one day per week of freelance or consulting work keeps your skills current, your professional identity alive, and your network active. It's often easier to return to full-time employment from freelancing than from a complete break. You might earn £200–400 per day, covering some costs while maintaining career continuity. This also gives you flexibility to work around childcare rather than against it – billing 6 hours when your partner is home, or working during naps and evenings.

Case Study: Lisa's Calculated Career Break

Pre-children: Lisa was earning £42,000 in a marketing role with a clear promotion track to senior manager within 18 months, which would have taken her salary to around £52,000.

Analysis: When Lisa calculated the costs of continuing to work with two children under three, the numbers were sobering. Childcare for both children would cost £24,000 annually, leaving her with just £9,600 net benefit after work expenses, or £800 per month. She'd essentially be working full-time for £4.62 per hour. The stress of managing two nursery drop-offs, a demanding job, and the inevitable childhood illnesses felt unsustainable. But simply quitting felt like throwing away a decade of career building.

Strategy – Negotiated 1-year sabbatical (unpaid but retained benefits): instead of resigning, Lisa approached her employer with a proposal for an unpaid sabbatical. She positioned this as a retention strategy – they'd keep a trained, experienced employee without recruitment costs, and she'd maintain her benefits (including her email address, access to systems, and company pension, even though she wasn't contributing, the account remained open). Having an official end date also meant she wasn't "out of the workforce" on her CV; she was on sabbatical, which is viewed very differently by future employers.

Used time for professional qualification (CIM Diploma): rather than framing her year as "time off," Lisa enrolled in the Chartered Institute of Marketing Diploma, which she'd been putting off for years due to workload. The course cost £2,400 and required roughly 8–10 hours of study per week, manageable around naps and evenings. This qualification immediately made her more valuable and opened doors to senior roles that had previously required it.

Maintained network through part-time consulting (1 day/week): Lisa reached out to her professional network and took on small consulting projects – social media audits, campaign strategy reviews, content planning.

She charged £300 per day and averaged 2–3 days per month, bringing in around £7,200 over the year. More importantly, this kept her LinkedIn active, her skills sharp, and her confidence intact. When she returned to job searching, she could demonstrate continuous professional activity.

Returned to promotion and £48k salary: when Lisa approached her employer about returning after her sabbatical year, the senior manager role she'd been tracking toward was available. With her new CIM Diploma, her consulting portfolio, and the fact that she'd stayed connected to the business informally, she was the obvious candidate. She returned not to her old £42,000 position, but to £48,000 in a more senior role – a 14% salary increase.

Outcome: Lisa's "career break" actually enhanced rather than hindered her progression. By the time her youngest started school three years later, she was earning £55,000 as a marketing director – a position she might not have reached so quickly had she stayed in her original role and burned out trying to juggle everything. The sabbatical year cost her £42,000 in lost salary, but the qualification, consulting income, and strategic positioning meant she more than recovered this within two years of returning. Most importantly, she avoided the resentment and exhaustion that often leads to permanent career exits. She describes it as "the best investment I made – I got time with my babies when they were tiny, gained a qualification I'd never have done otherwise, and came back stronger than I left."

Care Responsibilities: Financial Impact of Elderly Parent Care

Childcare responsibilities represent just one aspect of the caring roles that disproportionately affect women's financial lives. Increasingly, women find themselves in the 'sandwich generation', caring not only for children but also for aging parents. This dual caring responsibility creates another layer of financial complexity that we must acknowledge and plan for.

The Sandwich Generation Reality is that:

- 1 in 8 working adults provide care for elderly parents
- The average cost of care: £15,000–£40,000 annually per parent
- Career impact: 67% of carers reduce their working hours, 15% leave work entirely.

Financial Planning Strategies

Care cost forecasting can help with the assessment of the impact and cost of care. The following assessment framework can be used to consider this. It will of course be important to consider and discuss anything like this with wider family members:

- **Current health status:** Medical conditions, mobility, cognitive function
- **Care preferences:** Home care vs. residential preference

- **Financial resources:** Parent's assets, pension, savings
- **Family capacity:** Siblings' ability to contribute financially/practically.

The following 3 Bucket Approach can be a helpful approach to then follow:

Bucket 1 – Immediate Needs (0–2 years)

- Home adaptations: £3,000–£15,000
- Part-time care support: £200–£800/week
- Emergency fund: 3–6 months care costs
- Legal fees (LPAs, wills): £1,000 +

Bucket 2 – Medium-term Planning (2–10 years)

- Care home deposits: £25,000–£100,000
- Your income protection during reduced hours

Bucket 3 – Long-term Security (10+ years)

- Potential inheritance impact
- Your own care needs planning
- Pension contribution maintenance

Alongside this, consider your own income protection strategies to protect your financial position during this time through negotiating the option of flexible working arrangements with your employer. Here are some negotiation points that can be helpful to consider:

- Compressed hours (4.5 days instead of 5)
- Remote working options
- Carer's leave policies
- Emergency leave arrangements

In addition, make sure you look into the various financial support options that may be available to you, such as:

- Carer's Allowance: £76.75/week (if caring 35+ hours)
- Council support: Means-tested care funding
- NHS Continuing Healthcare: Free care for health needs
- Family financial planning: Sibling contribution agreements

Case Study: Margaret's Balanced Approach

Situation: Margaret's mother was diagnosed with early-stage dementia, and her father, while physically well, was struggling emotionally and practically to cope with the caregiving demands. Margaret felt torn between her responsibility to her parents and her career, which she'd worked hard to build.

Challenge: Living 200 miles away made regular visits exhausting and unsustainable. Margaret's demanding full-time role as a senior manager meant she was constantly firefighting between conference calls and family crises. She felt guilty when at work and anxious about her parents when at home. The distance made it impossible to pop in for appointments or respond quickly to emergencies, and the stress was affecting her health, her relationships, and her performance at work.

Financial Strategy:

1. Family meeting to agree care funding split (3 siblings): Margaret initiated an honest conversation with her two siblings about their parents' care needs and costs. They agreed to pool resources proportionally based on each person's financial capacity, rather than splitting everything equally. This removed resentment and established clear expectations from the start. They documented the agreement to avoid future misunderstandings.
2. Negotiated 4-day working week with 20% salary reduction: rather than leaving her job entirely, Margaret approached her employer with a proposal to work four days a week, freeing up Fridays for travel and care coordination. While the salary reduction was significant (around £12,000 annually), it allowed her to maintain her pension contributions, career progression, and professional identity, things she would have lost entirely if she'd resigned.
3. Used savings to fund immediate home adaptations (£8,000): Margaret used a portion of her emergency savings to install grab rails, improve lighting, and adapt her parents' bathroom to reduce fall risks. This upfront investment prevented costly care home placement in the short term and gave her father the confidence to manage longer at home. She viewed this as an investment in extending her parents' independence.
4. Set up joint account with siblings for ongoing care costs: the three siblings established a dedicated account where each contributed monthly for care expenses (initially £300 each). This covered a weekly cleaner, a gardener for heavy tasks, and a care coordinator. Having transparent, shared finances avoided awkward conversations about who was paying for what and ensured consistency of care regardless of who was available.

5. Arranged local care coordinator to manage day-to-day needs: Margaret hired a professional care coordinator who lived locally and could attend GP appointments, liaise with social services, coordinate tradespeople, and check in regularly. This person became the "eyes and ears" on the ground, dramatically reducing Margaret's mental load and the need for crisis-driven trips.

Outcome: Three years on, Margaret has been promoted at work and maintains a sustainable routine. Her mother is still at home with progressively increased support, and her father feels supported rather than isolated. Margaret's financial sacrifice (the reduced salary plus her savings contribution) totalled around £44,000 over three years, but this prevented a premature care home placement (average cost £40,000+ per year) and protected her career trajectory, which would have cost significantly more in lost earnings and pension over time. Most importantly, Margaret avoided burnout and maintained relationships with both her parents and her siblings. She describes the four-day week as "the best decision I made. I kept my career and my sanity, and Mum and Dad got better care than if I'd tried to do it all myself."

Implementation Roadmap

Immediate Actions (Next 30 Days)

1. **Salary Research:** Use 3 salary comparison tools for your role
2. **Pension Review:** Check current contribution levels and employer matching
3. **Care Assessment:** Evaluate elderly parents' current and future needs
4. **Childcare Audit:** Calculate true cost vs. income if applicable

Medium-term Planning (3–6 Months)

5. **Negotiation Preparation:** Develop salary negotiation strategy and documentation
6. **Pension Optimisation:** Implement salary sacrifice or additional contributions
7. **Care Planning:** Establish legal frameworks (LPA) and financial agreements
8. **Career Strategy:** Develop flexible working proposals

Long-term Security (1+ Years)

9. **Regular Reviews:** Annual assessment of all strategies
10. Contingency Planning: Scenario planning for major life changes
11. **Network Building:** Maintain professional connections during any career breaks
12. **Knowledge Updates:** Stay current with changing legislation and benefits

Understanding these gender-specific financial challenges isn't about accepting limitation, it's about strategic preparation. When you know the financial landscape, you can navigate it more effectively. Throughout this book, we'll return to these themes, providing specific strategies for each challenge we've identified here. In Chapter 3, we'll explore how to build the confidence needed to address these challenges head-on. In Chapter 12, we'll dive deep into protecting your pension during part-time work. And in Chapter 13, we'll tackle the salary negotiations that can help close these gaps. Your awareness of these challenges is the first step in your financial rebellion.

Chapter 2 Workbook Exercises: The Gender Money Gap

1. **Quick Knowledge Check:** True or False:
   - Women typically live 3–5 years longer than men ____________
   - Career breaks only affect current income, not pensions ____________
   - Women's investment timelines can actually be an advantage ____________

2. **One Key Reflection:**
   What gender-specific challenge will most impact my financial future?
   - ☐ Career breaks
   - ☐ Salary negotiation
   - ☐ Longevity planning
   - ☐ Confidence gaps
   - ☐ Other:

3. **Priority Action This Week:**
   - ☐ Calculate the potential impact of any planned career break
   - ☐ Research my state pension forecast
   - ☐ Schedule a conversation about financial expectations with my partner

Remember...

The gender money gap is real, but it's not insurmountable. Understanding these challenges allows us to plan more effectively and build stronger financial futures. In the next chapter, we'll explore how to build the confidence to take action on these plans, turning knowledge into power.

Chapter 3:
Building Your Money Confidence

"I'm successful in my career, I run a department of fifty people, and I can negotiate million-pound contracts. So why do I feel like an imposter when it comes to my own money?"

I hear words like these time and again. So, if this sounds familiar, you are not alone! These words highlight something I've witnessed repeatedly: being confident in one area of life doesn't automatically translate to financial confidence. The good news? Financial confidence can be built, step by step, just like any other skill.

The Confidence-Competence Loop

We can think of financial confidence like learning to ride a bike. You start wobbly, perhaps with training wheels, but each successful ride builds both your skills and your belief in yourself. Soon, you're not just riding – you're enjoying the journey.

This powerful cycle works in four stages:

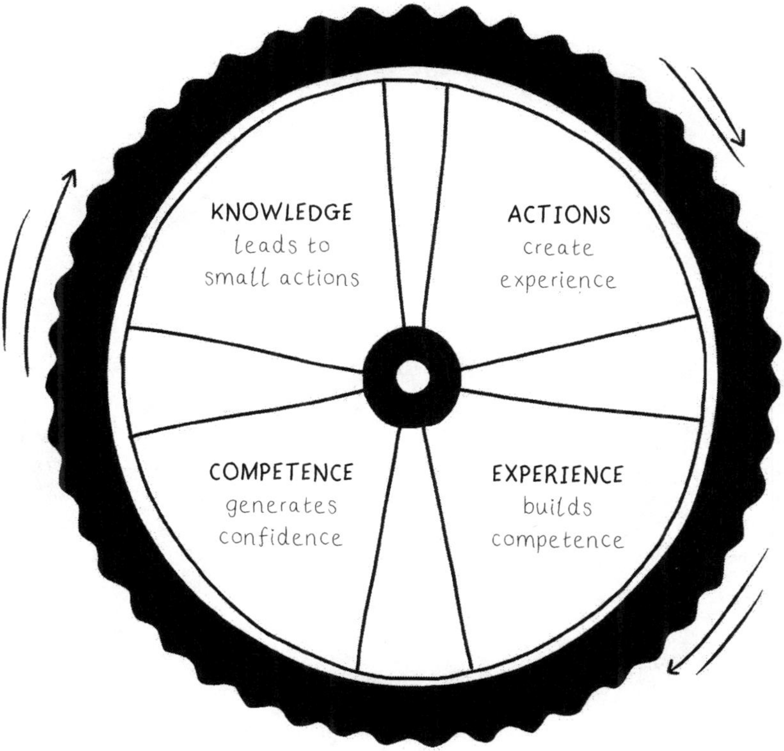

I have already talked about how powerful the human brain is and also how the brain looks for patterns and repeated behaviours to satisfy its need to keep you safe in the familiar. We've also learnt about our money personality. So, when we think about these simple 4 steps, we can see how they can help us to re-wire our money story and ultimately how we shape our future.

Let us pick an area to use as an example...

Investing is a subject that many women starting out in their financial journey want to understand better. I have found that this particular area of financial planning can lead to paralysis of action for lots of individuals, because it feels too big and overwhelming with a lack of knowledge about where to start.

So, using this as an example and applying the above framework to it:

- **Knowledge:** I know I need to start investing some of my money rather than leave it in cash to give it a chance to work harder for me over the longer term.
- **Action:** I will set up an investment account and start putting £x per month into it
- **Experience:** watching my investment grow over time builds my competence – I learn to stay invested during stock market downturns
- **Competence:** after some time of continuing to invest, experiencing how investments behave, I feel more confident and may start to look at other types of investments and opportunities.

Confidence is built by doing, not just from knowing.

QUICK CHECK-IN: What's one small financial action you could take this week to nudge your confidence up a notch?

Common Confidence Blockers

Let's talk about what stands in our way – and more importantly, how to move past it. Financial confidence isn't something most of us are born with. It's built through knowledge, experience, and often, through confronting the internal narratives that hold us back. These "blockers" aren't weaknesses or failures, they're deeply ingrained patterns that many of us carry, often without realising how much they're shaping our financial decisions. The good news? Once you can name them, you can challenge them.

External Blockers:

Conflicting Advice – Have you ever noticed how everyone has an opinion about money? Your colleague swears by property investment, your brother insists crypto is the future, and your friend says you're crazy if you're not in index funds. No wonder we feel overwhelmed! The key isn't finding the "perfect" advice – it's learning to evaluate information and make decisions that align with your goals.

Information Overload – There is so much information available at our fingertips. There are Finfluencers on every social media channel, there are self-help guides, there are courses, there are books, there are podcasts. Even when the information isn't conflicting, there is so much of it that it can become completely overwhelming. Sometimes we need the help of an external individual to help filter out the noise and focus on what actually matters for your situation.

Past Negative Experiences – Bad experiences with money can leave lasting scars. There are significant stock market moments, such as the 2008 financial crisis, that have impacted on individuals' confidence in investing. Without understanding the cause and the corresponding impact of the situation, it is easy to panic and withdraw your investments – at the worst possible time. This can leave you feeling anxious, upset and in extreme cases, never wanting to go there again!

Understanding that past experiences inform but don't dictate our future choices is crucial.

Internal Blockers:

Fear of Making Mistakes – "What if I make the wrong decision?" Have you ever thought this? I know I have. But here's the truth: there are very few truly irreversible financial decisions. Most "mistakes" can be learning opportunities if we frame them correctly.

Imposter Syndrome – This shows up in fascinating ways with money. I've worked with surgeons, CEOs, and barristers who feel like they should somehow inherently "know" about finance because they're successful in other areas. Let's be clear: financial knowledge is learned, not inherited. Don't punish yourself over what you haven't yet learnt.

If any of these areas have stood out to you where you've shouted a resounding 'yes', make a note of them. Either write some notes in the margin of the book or scribble your thoughts down in your journal. I would encourage you to reflect on them and to jot down what you think your next steps might be.

PAUSE HERE: Have you ever caught yourself thinking, "I should already know this"? Write down when that last happened.

Building Your Confidence Foundation

Financial confidence can be built. I've seen women's confidence grow as we've worked together and I want to distil some of this experience into your own financial confidence toolkit for you to carry with you and use at any time you need. So let's look at what you're going to put in your kit:

1. **Knowledge Building** – Start with the "need to know, nice to know" approach:
    - Need to know: Core concepts that affect your immediate financial decisions
    - Nice to know: Additional information that can wait until you're ready

Create your personal learning plan:

- Identify your preferred learning style (videos, reading, workshops?)
- Set aside regular learning time (even 15 minutes counts)
- Focus on one concept at a time
- Practice explaining concepts to others. This is a key step that we can easily skip over but this is the stage when the knowledge really embeds itself. It can often show us that where we thought we had grasped a concept, it is not perhaps quite to the depth we assumed and practicing explaining it can help us overcome this and secure our knowledge at a greater depth.

2. Decision-Making Skills – A great framework to help hone decision making skills is something that I call the "CLEAR" decision-making framework. Applying this approach to any decision making process helps to bring more awareness and intention to the process. This is how it works:

Collect relevant information

List the options and outcomes

Evaluate the pros and cons

Assess your comfort level

Review and adjust

Think about this with any major decision that you might have made or be faced with now. Often, it's not the decision itself that causes us worry; its worrying that that single decision is a make or break for something; it's not having a process for making decisions. Once they have a framework for how to approach their decision making, I have seen women's confidence soar.

3. Support Systems – There have been many studies which have shown that (in general) women place a high value on being able to discuss their challenges with others, rather than make decisions alone. We often stay more motivated to push on with change when we have encouragers around us cheering us on. If you have embarked on a fitness or weight loss program, I imagine most of us would consider a personalised fitness plan, gym membership or personal trainer. So why should financial fitness be any different? When you think about it like that, having a support system in place makes so much sense! Your support system might include:

- Professional advisers
- Money-savvy friends
- Learning communities
- Mentors who have walked your path

What sort of support system do you need in your life to help with your financial confidence and who might this be?

Confidence-Building Strategies by Money Personality

Your path to financial confidence will look different depending on your money personality archetype. Here's how to build on your natural strengths:

Status Seekers – Redefining Success Metrics: Your drive for achievement is a genuine strength. Channel it into building net worth rather than maintaining appearances. Track your investment growth with the same intensity you once tracked status purchases. Create "wealth-building status" goals – like reaching your first £10,000 invested or achieving a specific net worth milestone. Your competitive nature can be your greatest asset when directed toward real wealth building.

Guardians – Calculated Confidence: Your caution comes from wisdom, not weakness. Build confidence by starting with small, well-researched investments. Your natural research skills are perfect for due diligence. Set aside a small "learning investment" amount – perhaps £50–£100 monthly – to practice investing while your main savings remain secure. As you see this grow, your confidence will too.

Free Spirits – Values-Aligned Confidence: Connect your financial decisions to your values and confidence follows naturally. When your money aligns with what matters to you, you'll feel more engaged and committed. Consider sustainable investing options that match your generous spirit. Your enthusiasm for life becomes enthusiasm for your financial future when the two are connected.

Avoiders – Systems-Based Confidence: Confidence comes from having systems that work automatically, removing the need for constant decision-making. Start with one simple automation – perhaps an automatic savings transfer – and build from there. Each system you implement successfully proves you CAN handle money, just in your own way.

Chapter 3 Workbook Exercises: Building Your Money Confidence

1. **Quick Knowledge Check:** Rate your current confidence (1–10):
   - Making investment decisions: _____
   - Understanding financial products: _____
   - Negotiating financial terms: _____
   - Planning for long-term goals: _____

2. **One Key Reflection:** My biggest confidence blocker is:
   - ☐ Fear of making mistakes
   - ☐ Information overload
   - ☐ Past negative experiences
   - ☐ Imposter syndrome
   - ☐ Lack of support system

3. **Priority Action This Week:**
   - ☐ Read one financial article from a trusted source
   - ☐ Ask one financial question I've been avoiding
   - ☐ Practice explaining one money concept to someone else

Chapter 4:
Financial Wellbeing – The Connection Between Money and Life

We often assume that more money means less worry. A bigger salary, larger savings, a healthy pension – surely that should add up to peace of mind? But I've witnessed time and again working with clients across every income level that financial wealth doesn't automatically create financial wellbeing. In fact, I've met people earning six figures who lie awake worrying about money, while others on modest incomes sleep soundly.

Take Lisa, for example. On paper, she had everything: a six-figure salary, substantial savings, and a well-funded pension. Yet she couldn't sleep, felt constantly anxious about money, and struggled to enjoy her success. Lisa's story shows us why we need to talk about wellbeing, not just wealth.

The Five Dimensions of Financial Wellbeing

Financial Security

Financial security is the foundation of your financial wellbeing. It's not about having endless resources – it's about having enough to feel stable and protected. When women come to me asking for advice on any financial aspect, I always start with ensuring that we have reviewed their emergency cash fund to make sure they have a minimum of 3–6 months of expenses saved, before committing any further funds to investments. This is vital to ensure that any short term financial emergencies can be funded without causing a problem. It's also thinking about the hard questions; "what would my / my family's financial position be if something happened to me / my partner"? Financial security is a top concern for many of my clients and knowing there is insurance in place to protect the family if anything happens to them can be a huge relief. Hearing clients say "I am sleeping well again at night" following work in this area is not unusual.

Your security needs are personal to you. They will depend on your circumstances and also your values. Whilst there will be some commonalities, it is important for you to identify what it is that concerns you the most. It could be:

Emergency fund sizing

- Income stability planning
- Future needs assessment
- Risk management strategy

Once you have identified your needs, you can then go about tackling them, so you feel financially secure.

Financial Freedom

This is about choices – the ability to say yes (or no) based on what matters to you, not just what you can afford.

Catherine had always enjoyed her job, having worked hard and progressed to the role of Chief Operating Officer. But things had changed so much over the last few years that she realised she had gotten stuck on a treadmill she didn't feel she could get off. We talked about what she loved and what she didn't enjoy. She started to look at different career options and different ways of working. Some of them appealed, but there was also a big fear of leaving a secure position (even though she was no longer happy). We used the CLEAR framework (remember: Collect information, List the options, Evaluate pros and cons, Assess your comfort, Review and adjust) to work through these options. With that process, Catherine came to the place where she realised she wanted to leave the fast pace which came with city working and become a self-employed consultant, able to control her time and who she worked with. Together we created a "freedom fund" which allowed her enough financial security to be able to take a step into the financial unknown. For most women, freedom is not about never working again – it is about having options.

Here are some of the key areas to consider when contemplating what financial freedom might look like for you:

- Career flexibility
- Lifestyle choices
- Time management
- Location independence

Why not spend some time thinking about what financial freedom looks like for you?

	Looks to me like...
Career flexibility	
Lifestyle choices	
Time management	
Location independence	

Financial Peace of Mind

This dimension often surprises people. You can be wealthy and still lack peace of mind, or have modest means and feel completely at peace with your finances.

If you have ever been on one of my Money Personality workshops you will know that a big part of financial peace of mind is recognising your money personality and working with yourself, not constantly pushing against. This doesn't mean that if you love spending, you continue to spend beyond your means and not worry about the consequences. But what it does mean is that you recognise your personality type and then you create frameworks to work within that so that you don't starve yourself of the dopamine hit that you get when spending, but you create boundaries to do that within it in order to protect yourself and change the consequences.

Different elements will be the cause of worry or peace for each of us. Some of these can include:

- Stress reduction strategies
- Decision confidence
- Value alignment
- Mental clarity

Which of these, or anything else, is stealing your peace of mind right now?

Rachel, a high-earning consultant, achieved peace of mind not by earning more, but by finally aligning her spending with her values. "I stopped trying to keep up with everyone else's definition of success," she told me.

Financial peace of mind can bring such relief that it is not unusual for the results to spill over into other areas of your life (more energy or a new determination to start on that personal training program at the gym, or the confidence to enrol on that new course).

Financial Purpose

Money is a tool, not a destination. Understanding your financial purpose means knowing what you want your money to do for you and others. This can grow and develop with us through life. It is not about starting out in life with all these areas nailed and a clear plan which you never deviate from (although for some people that will happen). For most of us, we will discover more about ourselves as we walk through life. Some situations that we face we respond to in ways that we never dreamt we would. Our characters become moulded as we grow and respond to our circumstances. There may be times in our lives when our immediate situation is so all-consuming that we simply don't have the capacity to think beyond the now and putting one foot in front of the other. But whether you are early on in your life journey or well into those years and looking back at how life's twists and turns have shaped you, I encourage you to think about your purpose.

Here are some examples to explore, though you might find others that stand out for you:

- What are your personal values
- Legacy planning; what do you want to be remembered for or leave behind when you go
- Impact goals; is there something that impassions you to bring about change
- Meaningful contribution; is there a cause or a person(s) who you would love to impart to, that would make such a difference in their lives, either with your time, money or something else

When you have this clarity, it can make every financial decision more meaningful.

Financial Relationships

It is likely no surprise that money affects, and is affected by, our relationships. Understanding this dimension is crucial for overall wellbeing. This is not limited to your life partner, but can affect many different levels of relationships; house sharers, work partners, friends holidaying together.

I am going to use the example here of my own financial relationship with my husband. Each of us have our own money personalities. Each of us came from different financial backgrounds and we each had our own ideas of how we should be managing money. For us, after parenting challenges, our biggest relational challenges have been around managing money and what each of us deems to be a priority. This is because we each have our own values.

Over the years we have learnt what are essential priorities for each of us and what areas we are more willing to forego. For example, one year Simon felt very strongly that he wanted us to make a significant financial gift to someone. I didn't have the same emotional desire to do so, but I also wasn't against it. We talked through what it would mean for us as a family to give up in order to make this gift and came to an agreement on the value of the gift and together agreed to accept what the impact may then mean for us as a family (in terms of the lack of spending on ourselves that would mean for us that year). One of my fascinating observations from this time was how I then became emotionally invested in what we had together agreed to do. Not to the same extent as Simon, but it increased my awareness and willingness to invest in others.

In this example, if I hadn't been open to working with Simon on how much we were willing to give as a family and if Simon hadn't been willing to listen to me about my concerns around what the potential impact on our family could be and why that was important to me, then this situation could have ended quite differently. The key, as with any relationship, is having open communication and for both partners being willing to listen, not judge and willing to work together to find the right balance in the decision-making process.

Here are the areas which you may find helpful to focus on when considering your financial relationships. What do you need to do to increase your financial wellness in any of these areas?

	How healthy are these financial relationships?
Family dynamics	
Partnership communications	
Professional relationships	
Community connections	

QUICK CHECK-IN: Which of the five dimensions feels strongest for you right now? Which feels weakest?

The Mind-Money Connection

There is fascinating research that shows the same area of the brain is triggered when either money decisions are made, or physical threats or rewards are considered. Think about that for a minute. Money issues are one of the highest causes of relationship strains and when we understand how our brains respond to these conversations, we start to realise it's no wonder! When we start to understand the way our brain is wired to respond to money decisions, we can start to:

- Recognise what emotional triggers to look out for or be aware of
- Make better decisions under stress
- Build healthier money habits
- Improve our overall wellbeing

Creating Your Wellbeing Framework

One of the privileges of working with so many different women is that I have been able to witness the varied descriptions and meanings that we each give to money. It never fails to amaze me the different responses we each give to the same simple question "what does money mean to you"?

So, it won't surprise you to know that financial wellbeing therefore, whilst essential for us all, isn't universal. It's deeply personal.

One of the women I spoke with measured her financial success by how many months she could go without checking her bank account before making a purchase. For one of my friends, it's whether she can say yes for her kids to enrol in a sports club. For another client it is whether she can continue to fund her lifestyle and her future desires herself, without her husband's income. For another client, it's knowing that there is enough money to be able to call it a day and walk away from her workplace if she remains unhappy there.

Your financial wellbeing framework should reflect what matters to you.

What Does Financial Wellbeing Look Like for You?

Take a moment right now. If you're comfortable to, close your eyes and take a couple of deep breaths in and out. When you imagine feeling financially secure and at peace, what does that look like?

Is it waking up without that knot in your stomach about bills? Is it being able to help your aging parents without resentment? Is it knowing your children's education is covered? Or perhaps it's something as simple as buying fresh flowers every week without checking the price tag.

There are traditional steps that I would always recommend to any client as a matter of course (six months of emergency savings, paid-off debt, pension savings). These absolutely matter, but they're not the whole story. I've met millionaires who live in financial anxiety and teachers with modest salaries who feel content and without financial worry.

So, what are important factors for you with your own financial wellbeing? Here are some examples which you may find helpful to think about:

Security indicators: Beyond having an emergency fund, what makes you feel safe? Is it knowing you could continue to provide for your family if the unthinkable happened to your partner? Or is it having a varied source of income to reduce your dependency on a single source?

Freedom measures: What choices do you want to be available to you? Would it be the ability to choose to quit a job without financial worry, to relocate, travel, or to help family members in financial or practical ways?

Peace of mind markers: What financial situations currently trigger anxiety? Not having these triggers might be your true measure of success.

Purpose alignment: Does your money flow toward the things you value most? If your bank statements reflected your deepest values, would you recognise yourself?

Relationship health: How do financial decisions affect your important relationships? Financial wellbeing includes harmony around money with your partner, family, and friends.

Creating Goals That Actually Matter

It is all to easy to set goals that we think are great, but actually turn out to be arbitrary. What we find when we hit those goals (if we even stick with them and don't lose interest in the meantime) is often... nothing. No lasting satisfaction. Because arbitrary goals are usually based on chasing numbers, not feelings.

Often, I have seen goals that have transformed women's relationships with money. They were tied to what they wanted to feel and experience. So try thinking about this in a different way:

Short-term wins: What small financial victory would give you a genuine sense of accomplishment within the next 3 months? Maybe it's finally setting up that automatic transfer to savings that you've been meaning to do for years. Or having one completely guilt-free splurge that you've planned for and saved up or set aside designated funds for.

Medium-term progress: What financial change would genuinely improve your daily life within a year? Again this is so personal. I've seen clients plan and budget to save enough to take a sabbatical, a longer maternity leave or an early retirement.

Long-term vision: If money were no object, what would your life look like in 5–10 years? Close your eyes and really see it. Now, what's one financial step that moves you in that direction? Write it down in bold letters in the margin of this book!

Building Habits That Stick (Without Making Yourself Miserable)

I know that for many women, the prospect of financial advice before they work with me, can feel like dieting. Deprivation. Willpower. Guilt. And we all know how well most diets work long-term.

We are each experts in prescribing guilt for ourselves. It is something that I find deeply saddening because guilt can be crippling and so often there is absolutely no justified reason for it (although we may well have convinced ourselves it is justified!).

Sustainable financial habits aren't about perfect discipline. They're about knowing yourself well enough to set up systems that work with your quirks, not against them:

- **Regular financial reviews that don't make you want to gouge your eyes out:** Not everyone loves spreadsheets, so why not implement "Money Mondays"; 5 minutes with your favourite tea, checking one financial area each week (sometimes with chocolate!).
- **Mindful spending that doesn't feel like punishment:** Rather than cutting out shopping, put in place a "48-hour crush rule"; pop it in the basket and leave it there. If you're still thinking about it two days later, it might be love, not just lust!
- **Stress management techniques that acknowledge reality:** Financial stress happens. Having pre-planned responses (that aren't "shop till you drop" or "ignore all bills") makes a difference. My friend Emily keeps a "financial stress kit" with her favourite free activities for these moments to help remove the thought process at the time which can then turn into a negative spiral.

- **Relationship check-ins that build intimacy, not resentment:** Money talks with a partner can carry the risk of causing tension and arguments. Many clients I have worked with have implemented "financial date nights" on a regular basis. They create a warm environment – go out for coffee, cook a favourite dinner, make sure the children aren't going to interrupt, open a bottle of wine (but limit how much you will drink to help keep the conversation at a reasonable level) and are conscious about keeping the conversation gentle about where things are and where they're headed.

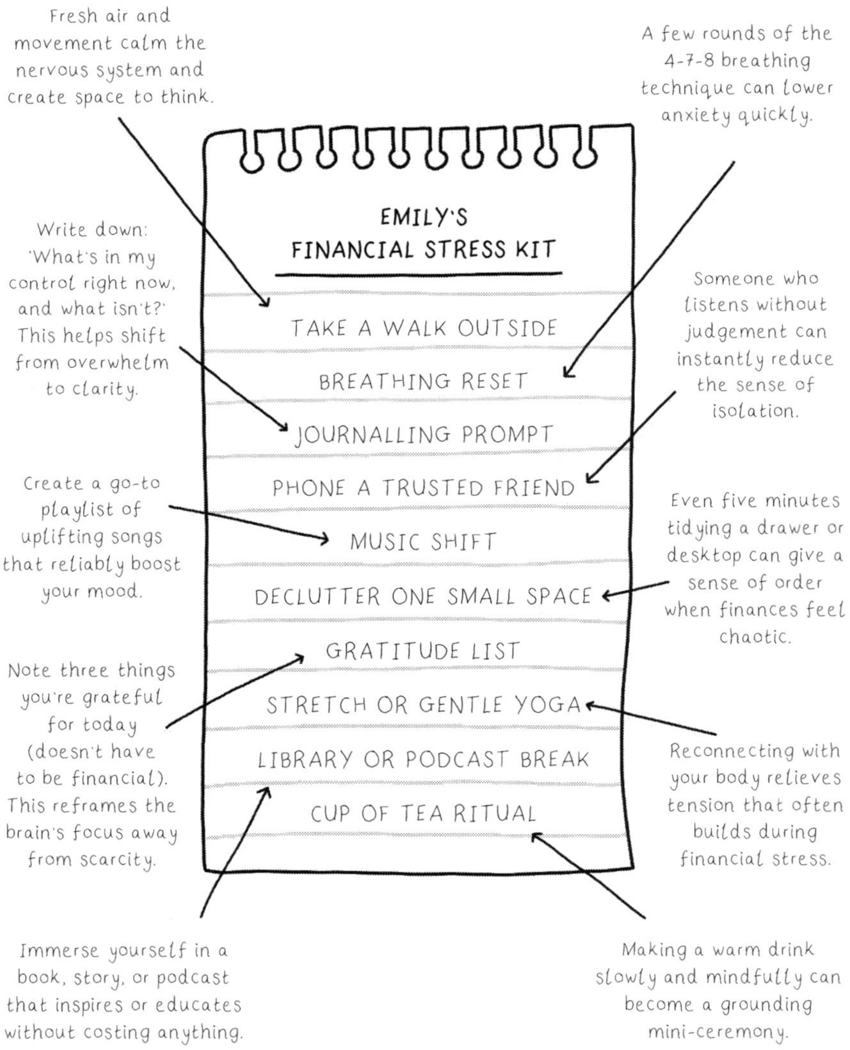

PAUSE HERE: If you had to create your own "stress kit," what's one free activity you'd include?

Remember, financial wellbeing isn't a destination. It's an ongoing relationship with yourself and your resources. Like any important relationship, it requires attention, honesty, and compassion, especially when things get messy. Because they will get messy. Life happens. Markets crash. Emergencies arise. Plans fall apart. Your framework needs to be flexible enough to bend without breaking, and forgiving enough that you can always begin again.

So, what does financial wellbeing look like for you? Not for your parents, your friends, or the experts, but for YOU?

That's where we start.

Chapter 4: Workbook Exercises: Financial Wellbeing

1. **Quick Knowledge Check:** Rate each dimension of your financial wellbeing (1–10):
   - Security: _____
   - Freedom: _____
   - Peace of Mind: _____
   - Purpose: _____
   - Relationships: _____

2. **One Key Reflection:** Financial wellbeing to me means:

3. **Priority Action This Week:**
   - ☐ Identify one financial stress I can address immediately
   - ☐ Set up one system to improve my financial organisation
   - ☐ Practice one mindful money moment before making a purchase

Moving Forward

Understanding your own money story, recognising the gender-specific challenges that we face, building confidence, and focusing on wellbeing creates a powerful foundation for being able to then explore and implement practical financial skills.

Your financial journey is unique to you. Take what resonates, adapt what needs adjusting, and keep in mind that every step forward, no matter how small, counts.

Part 2: Essential Money Management

"Discipline is freedom in disguise." - Toni Morrison

Once we understand the emotional side of money, it's time to roll up our sleeves and get practical. Part 2 gives us the essential toolkit for day-to-day financial security; managing cash flow, building an emergency fund, understanding debt, and protecting our future. Think of this section as your financial "safety net." When we get these foundations in place, we remove stress, gain clarity, and create the stability we need to grow. It's about moving from confusion to control.

Chapter 5:
Taking Control of Your Cash Flow

Here's something I want you to let percolate for a minute or two and see what you think...

You can't manage what you don't measure.

For some, this is already securely nailed. If so, fantastic. For others, it's a real sticking point. If you're constantly wondering where your money goes each month, it's time to take control of your cash flow.

Understanding Your Money's Journey

If you're a visual learner, think of your finances like a river. Money flows in (your income) and flows out (your expenses). The goal isn't to dam the river completely – that's neither realistic nor enjoyable. Instead, we want to direct the flow where it needs to go, at the pace we want it to flow, as much as possible.

Before we dive in, here's a quick win you can do today:

Log into your banking app and scroll back through the last 7 days. Circle (or screenshot) any expense you'd completely forgotten about. You'll be amazed how often these slip through.

Now, for the full picture, you need to know exactly what's coming in and going out.

THE BRAIN & BUDGET BLINDNESS

Our brains are wired to pay more attention to big, dramatic changes than to small, repeated ones. That's why a £3 coffee barely registers, but the sum of 200 coffees a year (over £600) can feel shocking when tallied. Psychologists call this "denominator neglect", we notice single events but struggle to perceive their cumulative impact. Tracking helps make the invisible visible.

Step 1: Track Everything for 30 Days

Yes, everything. That £4 coffee, the 99p app, the contactless payment you've already forgotten about.

Here are some suggestions for how to do this, but use whatever method works for you (we also help you with this in our Eva Essential programme):

- Banking app
- Spreadsheet
- Notebook
- Budgeting app

The tool doesn't matter. Consistency does.

Step 2: Categorise Your Spending

Once you've got a month's worth of data, sort it into categories. Add a surprising or specific example to each – it helps make the numbers real:

- **Fixed essentials:** Rent, utilities, council tax (or that annual TV licence fee you only remember when the reminder arrives)
- Variable essentials: Groceries, transport (plus the odd taxi home in the rain)
- **Debt payments:** Credit cards, loans
- **Savings and investments:** ISA contributions, workplace pension top-ups
- **Lifestyle choices:** Entertainment, eating out, shopping (yes, that pair of "it was in the sale" shoes)

This is usually where people have their "oh sh'#" moment. That daily coffee habit? It can easily add up to £60+ a month. Those little Amazon purchases? These could be more like hundreds of pounds a month!

Remember, this is not a moment of judgement. It's the start of taking control and defining your future direction.

QUICK CHECK-IN: Did one category surprise you with how much you're spending? Circle it now.

Creating Your Cash Flow System

Option 1: The Four-Account System

- Current Account: Where your salary lands
- Bills Account: For all fixed expenses
- Spending Account: For variable expenses and fun money
- Savings Account: For your future self

How it works:

- Salary hits your current account
- Automatically transfer bill money to bills account
- Move your allocated spending money to your spending account
- Send savings to savings account
- Anything left in the current account is your buffer – a little reward for your efforts!

Option 2: The 50/30/20 Framework

If percentages are more your style, this one's simpler to implement:

- 50% needs (essentials you can't live without)
- 30% wants (things that make life enjoyable)
- 20% savings and debt repayment

These are guidelines, not gospel. Life stage and location matter. If you're living in London, for example, your "needs" might be 60%+ for now. If you're buying your first home or raising a family then that's a season where essentials might eat a bigger slice. The point is to start with awareness and adjust as your situation changes. It's being conscious of your allocations and adjusting with intention.

Plugging the Leaks

Think of financial leaks like a dripping tap. Individually, the drips seem small, but over time they quietly empty your account. Put the plug in and you'll see how much faster your "bath" fills. Never under-estimate the power of this exercise. Today's digital-first accounts have made this much easier to see with the benefits of 'rounding up' spending into savings. Here are some actions you can take to really start to see some benefits.

Subscription Audit

- List every subscription
- Used it in the last 3 months? If no, cancel it.
- If yes, ask: "Is it worth the cost?"

Mindful Spending Pause

Before any non-essential purchase, wait 24 hours. Still want it? Wait another 24. Still want it? Go ahead.

Bill Negotiation

- Call providers annually
- Mention competitor offers
- Ask about loyalty discounts
- Be willing to switch

QUICK CHECK-IN: Already thought of at least one leak to fix? Write it down now.

Unpredictable Income

If you're self-employed or have variable income, budgeting is trickier, but not impossible.

1. Work out your annual, monthly, and quarterly costs.
2. Break down irregular expenses into monthly "set-asides."
3. Use a cautious allocation method (in other words, over-estimate rather than under-estimate) so your essentials are always covered.

Example Table (3-month cycle):

Month	Income	Essentials	Set-Aside for Quarterly Costs	Remaining
1	£2,500	£2,000	£500	£0
2	£2,000	£2,000	£0	£0
3	£3,000	£2,000	£500	£500

Making It Sustainable

The best system is the one you'll actually stick to.

- **Automate everything possible** – bills, savings, transfers.
- **Build in fun money** – budget for treats so it's not all restriction.
- **Review regularly** – monthly money date, quarterly deep dive, annual MOT.

If you're worried you won't keep it up, find an accountability partner. This isn't weakness, it's how humans work best.

Growing up, one of the habits my dad taught me, which has stuck with me, is that for any bonus I received (which was therefore on top of my essential needs), to split it as follows:

- 40% off any debt (e.g., a mortgage overpayment)
- 40% to savings (e.g., a long term pot such as a pension)
- 20% for immediate reward and spending

Again, this isn't a rule and the percentages can change, but the principle of splitting out any additional income in this way has served me well over the years.

Budgeting Approaches by Money Personality

Different archetypes need different approaches to cash flow management. There's no one-size-fits-all budget. The above is a framework, but it's important that you find the approach that works with your natural tendencies. Try considering the following according to your dominant archetype:

Status Seekers – The Achievement Budget:
Create a "wealth-building status" category in your budget. Allocate funds for investments that build real net worth alongside limited spending on meaningful status items. Track your net worth monthly like a business KPI. Your goal: make your investment gains more impressive than any purchase.

Example: £500 monthly to investments, £200 to "meaningful status" (quality items that last), rather than £700 on lifestyle inflation.

Guardians – The Security Buffer Budget:
Build multiple savings categories: emergency fund, short-term goals, long-term growth. Your natural tendency to save can be channelled into strategic wealth building. Create specific pots for different purposes so you can see your security building across multiple areas.

Example: 30% of income to various savings categories (10% emergency, 10% short-term goals, 10% investments), giving you multiple layers of security.

Free Spirits – The Freedom Budget:

Use the 60–20–20 rule: 60% for needs, 20% for savings/investments, 20% for freedom spending. Automate the first two so your spontaneous nature can enjoy the third guilt-free. This gives you structure without feeling restricted.

Example: Automatic transfers handle the boring stuff, leaving you with a generous "joy budget" you can spend however feels right in the moment.

Avoiders – The Automatic Budget:

Set up three automatic transfers on payday: bills, savings, and spending money. Minimal decision-making required once the system is in place. Your mantra: "Set it and forget it." Check in quarterly, not daily.

Example: On payday, money automatically splits three ways. You only interact with your spending account day-to-day.

Chapter 5 Workbook Exercises: Taking Control of Your Cash Flow

1. **Quick Knowledge Check:** My current savings rate is approximately ____% of my income. (Don't know? That's your first action!)

2. **One Key Reflection:** My biggest cash flow challenge is:
   - ☐ Not knowing where money goes
   - ☐ Irregular income
   - ☐ Too many subscriptions
   - ☐ Emotional spending
   - ☐ No budget system

3. **Priority Action This Week:**
   - ☐ Track every expense for 7 days
   - ☐ Cancel one unused subscription
   - ☐ Set up one automatic transfer to savings

Final Nudge

Decide today which system (or mix of systems) you'll try first. Schedule your first "money date" in your diary before you finish reading. Your future self will thank you and so will your bank balance.

Chapter 6:
Building Your Safety Net

Life has a funny way of throwing curveballs when you least expect them. Your car breaks down. The boiler gives up in January. Your laptop dies the night before a big deadline.

Sound familiar?

These moments often arrive with bad timing and if we're not financially prepared, they can tip us into stress, debt, or sleepless nights. We can't always stop these things from happening, but we can protect ourselves from the financial shockwaves they cause.

That's where your safety net comes in giving you the breathing space to deal with life's surprises without panic.

The Emotional "Why" Behind a Safety Net

I can give you all the practical steps (and I will), but first, let's talk about what this is really about. It's not just about "being sensible" or "saving for a rainy day."

It's about:

- Sleeping well, knowing you could handle the unexpected without panic.
- Making decisions based on what's right for you, not what your bank balance dictates in the moment.
- Being able to help yourself and others when needed, without compromising your own stability.

When you have an emergency fund, you move through life differently. You're not living in the shadow of "what if?" and that is incredibly empowering.

The Emergency Fund: Your Financial Airbag

An emergency fund isn't a nice-to-have, it's essential. When I meet with clients, whether they're multi-millionaires or just starting out, this is the first thing I check. It's one of the key foundations of financial health, and it can be the difference between a minor inconvenience and a full-blown financial crisis.

So, what actually counts as an "emergency"? It's tempting to raid savings for a holiday deal or the latest phone, but that's not what this fund is for. Real emergencies are things that genuinely threaten your wellbeing or financial stability, such as:

- Job loss
- Unexpected medical expenses
- Critical home repairs
- Essential car repairs
- Things that we really aren't emergencies:
- Holiday deals
- Shopping sales
- Birthday presents
- Latest tech release

How Much Do You Need?

You'll often hear the advice to save 3–6 months of essential expenses, and that's a solid target. But it can feel daunting if you're starting from zero, so I we can break it down into stages:

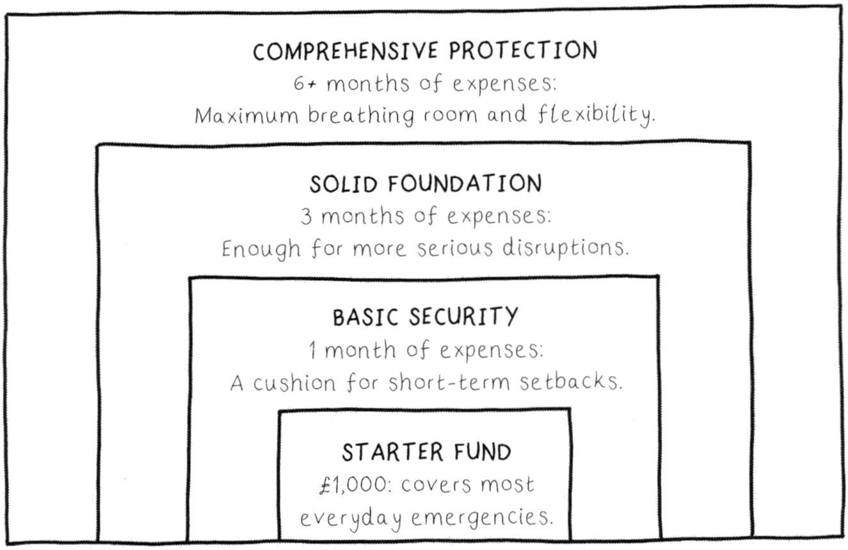

Don't get stuck on the final number, start where you are. If you've already worked through your budget and spotted areas where you can free up money, you've got the first building blocks ready.

My Own Emergency Fund Story

A few years ago, in the week before Christmas, our fridge broke down. Not a minor "it's making a funny noise" break, I mean dead and gone. Irreparable. The worst part? We had a house full of family arriving (we tend to host a lot of family at Christmas!), and it was completely stocked with Christmas food.

Because we had an emergency fund, we were able to replace it immediately – no stress, no debt, no frantic "how will we pay for this?" conversations. Instead of ruining our Christmas, it became a brief inconvenience and a slightly funny family story.

That's the power of a safety net. It turns potential disasters into manageable moments.

Building Your Fund From Scratch

If you're thinking, "I can barely make ends meet as it is," I do hear you. The truth is, most people start small and build over time. The key is consistency. Here are some simple, low-pressure ways to begin:

- **The Penny Challenge** – On day one, save 1p. Day two, save 2p. Day three, save 3p. Keep going for a year and you'll have £667.95 without really feeling it.
- **The Round-Up Method** – Use an app that rounds up your spending to the nearest pound and saves the difference. Buy a coffee for £3.50? 50p goes into your savings. These small amounts add up surprisingly quickly.
- **The Side Hustle Strategy** – Dedicate income from something extra (e.g., dog walking, tutoring, freelancing) straight to your emergency fund so it doesn't get absorbed into daily spending.
- **The Cut-One-Thing Approach** – Drop just one regular expense (a streaming service, takeaway coffee, unused subscription) and redirect that money to savings.

Psychological Traps to Avoid

- **"I'll start when I have more".** If you wait for the "perfect" time, it may never come. Start with what you have – even £5 matters.
- **Using a credit card as your emergency fund.** It's not the same. Debt adds financial pressure when you're already dealing with a crisis.
- **Dipping in for non-emergencies.** Buying a last-minute outfit for a party is not an emergency. Protect your fund by defining your own "emergency rules" in advance.

Where to Keep Your Emergency Fund

Your emergency fund needs to be:

- **Accessible** – You don't want to wait weeks to get your hands on it.
- **Separate** – Keep it away from your everyday spending account to avoid temptation.
- **Safe** – No market risk; this is about security, not investment returns.

The best options for an emergency fund are:

- Instant access savings account
- Cash ISA
- Premium Bonds (for larger amounts)

Don't obsess over the highest interest rate. The priority is that it's separate and available when you need it.

Beyond Emergency: Sinking Funds

Once you've got your emergency fund in place, it's time to think ahead to predictable expenses – the ones we know are coming but often forget to plan for. These are called sinking funds, and they can take so much stress out of your year.

Think about:

- **Christmas** – Saving a little each month means no January credit card hangover.
- **Car Costs** – MOT, servicing, repairs.
- **Holidays** – Set a realistic budget and stick to it.
- **Home Maintenance** – Boiler service, redecorating, repairs.
- **Annual Bills** – Insurance, memberships, birthdays.

To work out how much to save, total the yearly cost for each and divide by 12. You can keep them all in one "Annual Bills" account or have separate pots for each, whatever helps you stay organised and resist dipping into them.

For me, using sinking funds, removes a huge part of the stress of budgeting for big events like Christmas and family holidays. Instead of bracing myself for the December hit, I build the cost into my year so, financially speaking, Christmas comes and goes without the stress associated with costs that haven't been budgeted for. It can be a small shift for some of us and a huge mindset change for others, but the feeling of relief it can bring is not insignificant.

Life Stages: How Your Safety Net Changes

Your safety net will change over time, as your needs and circumstances adjust.

- **Starting Out:** lower living costs might mean a smaller fund is fine. Focus on building the habit.
- **Mid-Career / Family Life:** higher expenses and dependents mean you'll want a larger cushion.
- **Approaching Retirement:** prioritise stability and income predictability; aim for the upper end of the range.

The big takeaway?

Your safety net isn't about hoarding money "just in case." It's about buying yourself peace of mind, choice, and resilience. When you have it in place, you can face life's curveballs with calm instead of panic. That confidence ripples outward: you make better investment decisions, negotiate more boldly, and sleep more soundly. Your safety net doesn't just protect you from emergencies, it transforms how you show up to every financial decision.

Chapter 6 Workbook Exercises: Building Your Safety Net

1. **Quick Knowledge Check:** How many months of expenses could your current emergency fund cover?
   - ☐ Less than 1 month
   - ☐ 1–3 months
   - ☐ 3–6 months
   - ☐ 6+ months
   - ☐ Don't have one

2. **One Key Reflection:** An emergency fund would give me peace of mind because:

3. **Priority Action This Week:**
   - ☐ Calculate exactly how much I need for 3 months of essential
   - ☐ Open a separate savings account for emergencies
   - ☐ Set up an automatic transfer of £____ per week to my emergency fund

Chapter 7:
Understanding Good vs Bad Debt

Debt is something most of us will face at some point in our lives. In my experience it is a highly emotive subject and something that many of us label ourselves by. So, it's important that we understand the different types of debt and when and why they may either be helpful, or should be avoided.

I once worked with a client who told me she "hated debt." To her, it was a four-letter word that meant failure. Yet as we talked about the things most important to her, her home came straight to the top of the list, not just as a place for her children, but as a welcoming space where friends and family could simply come and be. She had a vivid picture of how she wanted it to feel.

She shared how honoured she felt to be living that dream and as we dug deeper, we established it was only possible because she had borrowed money through a mortgage to buy her home. In that moment, something shifted. She saw that debt could be both a force for good as well as for harm, having only really acknowledged the latter before. Her mortgage wasn't a burden; it was a tool that had made her vision possible.

So why did she feel so differently about her mortgage compared to the credit card balance that kept her awake at night? The answer is this: debt itself isn't inherently "good" or "bad." It's the purpose of the debt, the cost of it, and the impact it has on your life that matters. Some debt can be a springboard to your future. Some can be a ball and chain. And some sits somewhere in between.

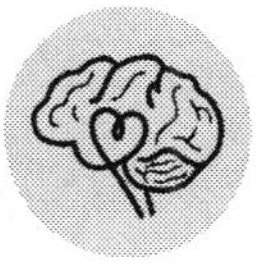

WHY DEBT FEELS LIKE QUICKSAND

Carrying debt activates the brain's threat system (similar to how we respond to danger). This can create avoidance behaviour, we don't open bills, we stop checking accounts. Ironically, the very avoidance meant to reduce stress makes the problem worse. Recognising the fight-or-flight response helps you pause, take a breath, and approach debt with a calmer, problem-solving mindset.

Good Debt: The Investment in Your Future

Think of good debt as a ladder, something you climb to reach new opportunities. It's the kind that helps you build assets, boost your income, or increase your skills.

Good debt often:

- Increases your net worth
- Generates income
- Enhances your earning potential
- Has relatively low interest rates
- Sometimes comes with tax benefits

Examples of good debt:

- **Student loans** – Investing in your education can open doors that might otherwise stay closed.
- **Mortgages** – Often the only route onto the property ladder, helping you build equity over time.
- **Business loans** – Funding a start-up or expanding a profitable business.
- **Professional development loans** – Gaining qualifications or skills that improve your earning power.

Many women I have worked with have decided to retrain during their working lives. It has often been necessary to take on some level of debt in order to do this. Without this facility, the cost of retraining is not always affordable as quickly as the debt might facilitate. Following completion of the qualification or training, earnings potential, career progression or satisfaction will often grow at a rate faster than had the debt not been accessed. This won't always be the right route for everyone, but where this can work, it is a great example to show that not all debts are necessarily 'bad'.

Good debt is something that, under normal circumstances, should remain well within your control and be a facilitator for something you have planned for.

Bad Debt: The Wealth Drainer

Bad debt is the treadmill; lots of effort, but you stay in the same place. It's expensive, doesn't add value, and often funds short-term wants rather than long-term needs.

Bad debt often:

- Decreases your value
- Has high interest rates
- Doesn't generate income
- Fuels lifestyle spending instead of investment

Examples of bad debt:

- **Credit card debt** for non-essentials
- **Payday loans** with extreme interest rates
- **Car loans** for vehicles far beyond your means
- **Store cards** with high rates and limited use

Left unchecked, bad debt can quietly grow until it becomes overwhelming and emotionally exhausting. This is the area of debt I hear talked about the most when stories are exchanged between individuals sharing "what a mess" they have gotten into and with these stories the over-riding sense of shame that is carried.

The Grey Area

Not all debt fits neatly into "good" or "bad." Some debts are situational, helpful if they are managed well, but harmful if not. Here are some examples:

- **Car loans** – Essential for work? Affordable within your budget? Could be a practical choice.
- **0% credit cards** – Useful for spreading the cost of large purchases if you clear the balance before interest kicks in.
- **Personal loans** – Fine if the terms are fair and the purpose is aligned with your goals.

PAUSE HERE: For each of your debts, ask "is this helping me move forward, or is it holding me back?"

Remember, it's the purpose of the debt, the cost of it, and the impact it has on your life that matters.

Taking Back Control of Debt

When debt feels heavy, I always start with the same question:
Are you in control of your debt, or is your debt controlling you?

If you are feeling even just a little bit out of control, here's a helpful framework to walk through that can help you regain control of your debt:

1. **Get it all out in the open**
   - List every debt: lender, balance, interest rate, minimum payment, due date, and whether it's good, bad, or grey area.

2. **Choose your repayment approach**
   - **Avalanche method** – Focus on the highest-interest debt first while paying minimums on the rest. This saves you the most money overall.
   - **Snowball method** – Focus on the smallest balance first for quick wins and momentum.

3. **Accelerate the process**
   - Round up payments so you chip away at the balance faster.
   - Put any windfalls (bonuses, refunds, extra income) straight towards debt.
   - Consider 0% balance transfers (watch out for the fees though).
   - In some cases, consolidation with expert guidance can simplify and reduce costs.

Using Credit Wisely

Credit is a tool, not a moral judgment. It can accelerate your goals or sabotage them. The difference is understanding how and when to use it.

Benefits of using credit well:

- Purchase protection on big buys
- Rewards or cashback
- Builds your credit history
- Interest-free periods to help spread costs

PAUSE HERE: Golden rule – Pay in full each month (or before the interest-free period ends).

SNOWBALL METHOD

1. Focus on smallest balance first
2. Maintain minimums on the remaining balances
3. Once cleared, roll payment into the next debt

This will provide quick wins & strong momentum

AVALANCHE METHOD

1. Focus on highest interest debt first
2. Maintain minimums on the remaining balances
3. Once cleared, move on to the next highest rate

This will provide the biggest financial saving overall

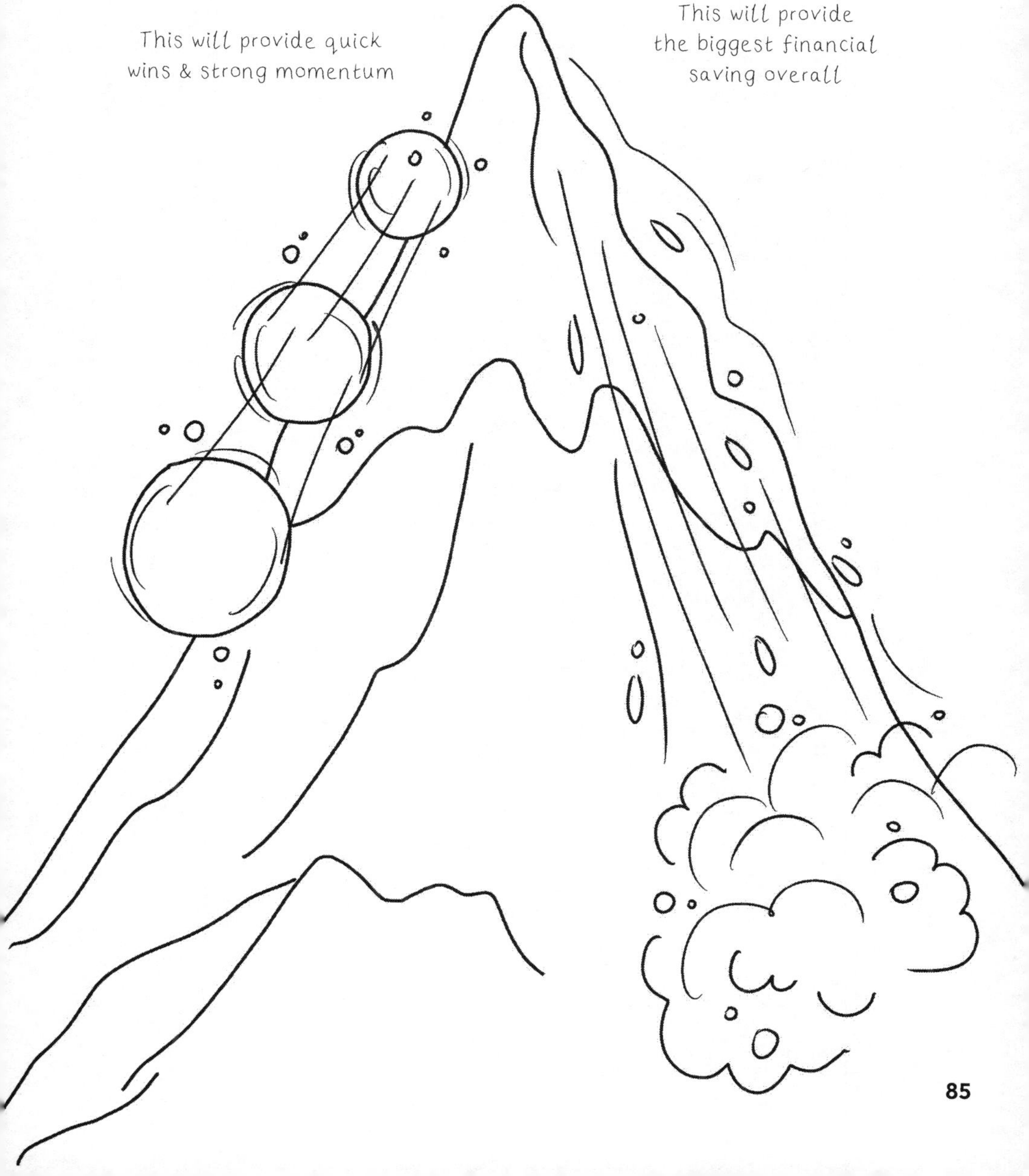

Eva Explains: Understanding Credit Scores and Applications

Your credit score is like a snapshot of your borrowing history, showing how you've managed things like credit cards, loans, and even mobile phone contracts. Lenders use it, along with your income and other factors, to decide whether to offer you credit.

If you've ever been declined for credit (for example, an iPad payment plan), it can feel confusing, but here's what's important to know:

Being declined doesn't damage your credit score. The decision is based on the lender's internal criteria, not a mark against you.

The credit check carried out during your application might leave a small "hard search" footprint on your file. This can very slightly reduce your score for a short time, but only if you make multiple applications close together.

Checking your own score is completely safe. It's known as a soft search and has no impact on your credit rating.

You can check your score for free with:

- Experian – experian.co.uk
- Equifax (via ClearScore) – clearscore.com
- TransUnion (via Credit Karma) – creditkarma.co.uk

If you've been declined, try:

- Checking your credit report for any outdated or incorrect information
- Ensuring you're on the electoral roll at your current address
- Making at least the minimum payments on any existing credit
- Avoiding several applications within a short period

Remember, a decline doesn't mean you've done anything wrong. Sometimes it's simply about the lender's internal rules or affordability checks. A little curiosity and a credit report review are all it takes to understand what's really going on.

Building Good Credit Habits

Healthy credit habits open doors to better rates, easier approvals, and more flexibility. This can be helpful to build for when you may need to access debt to help with your overall financial planning. You can help yourself by:

- Register to vote (in the UK, this can boost your credit score)
- Paying all bills on time
- Keep credit utilisation under 30% (e.g., so if you have a credit card with a £5,000 limit you'd only want to use up to £1,500 of this limit. This is because this shows the lender that you have access to credit but don't rely too heavily on it, which can help to build your credit score)
- Avoid multiple applications close together
- Check your credit report regularly

When to Ask for Help

If you're only making minimum payments, relying on credit for essentials, losing sleep over money, or getting calls from collectors please know you're not alone. If you have followed the framework outlined above and still feel that you aren't fully in control then it may be time to seek further help.
As at the time of writing, the following sources offer free, confidential help:

- StepChange
- Citizens Advice
- National Debtline
- Money Advice Service

And remember, debt is often linked to your money story. Sometimes, a few sessions with a financial coach or therapist can help untangle old patterns and give you a fresh start.

Chapter 7 Workbook Exercises: Understanding Good vs Bad Debt

1. Quick Knowledge Check: Which of these is typically "good debt"?

- ☐ Credit card for holiday
- ☐ Mortgage
- ☐ Store card
- ☐ Payday loan

2. One Key Reflection: My current debt situation makes me feel:

- ☐ In control
- ☐ Slightly worried
- ☐ Overwhelmed
- ☐ Proud of my progress

3. Priority Action This Week:

- ☐ List all my debts with balances and interest rates
- ☐ Identify one "bad debt" to pay off first
- ☐ Calculate how much extra I could pay toward debt monthly

Moving Forward

Debt doesn't have to be a source of shame. It's simply a tool; one that can work for you or against you.

This week, take an honest look at every debt you have and sort them into three columns: Ladders (helping you climb), Treadmills (keeping you stuck), and Grey Area. Decide on your next steps for each, starting small if you need to.

The goal here isn't perfection, it's progress. Awareness gives you choice. And choice gives you power.

Chapter 8:
Protection – Securing Your Financial Future

Over the years, one of the most common things I hear from women is that they lie awake at night worrying about what their situation would be like if something happened to their partner. Not the "I-can't-find-the-remote" kind of worry, the deep, stomach-churning kind that keeps you staring at the ceiling at 2am and desperately trying not to think about it the rest of the time.

Would the mortgage still get paid? Could they keep the house? How would they manage financially?

Playing through the "what if" scenarios is not uncommon. It doesn't necessarily mean that you are expecting disaster, but in many cases the women I speak to say it's that they don't know what would happen if it came.

Here's the good news: for something that causes so much anxiety, the financial solution is often surprisingly straightforward.

Insurance.

Now, I know, that word doesn't exactly set your pulse racing. It's up there with "tax return" and "root canal" on the excitement scale. But stay with me! Because the right protection isn't about selling policies or making insurance companies richer – it's about buying yourself peace of mind.

All insurance is just that – a payment to provide for you in the event of something happening (holiday insurance to cover the cost of a flight being cancelled, car insurance to cover the cost of repairing the car in an accident…). The reason I think the right insurance is so important; it's knowing that if the unthinkable happened, you wouldn't be making big financial decisions while in emotional freefall. You'd have the breathing space, the security, and the resources to focus on yourself and your loved ones.

Think of protection as your financial immune system. You hope you never need it, but you'll be grateful it's there if you do.

The Protection Hierarchy

I like to think of protection in layers, a bit like Maslow's hierarchy of needs, but for your money.

Level 1: Emergency Fund

We've already covered this. It's your first line of defence for those "life-happens" moments (broken boilers, dental emergencies, and car breakdowns).

Level 2: Essential Insurance

This is the non-negotiable stuff. Health insurance (if you're outside the UK or without NHS access), car insurance (because it's the law), home insurance (buildings and contents), and life insurance (if you have dependents or a mortgage).

Level 3: Income Protection

This one often gets overlooked, yet it protects your biggest asset – your ability to earn. It can replace a portion of your income if you can't work, often until you retire.

Think about this situation; Emma, a freelance consultant, broke her leg badly in a skiing accident. She had built an emergency fund (big tick!) and assumed her savings would get her through. Six months later, her emergency fund had vanished, and she was relying on credit cards. Emma's sentiments; "I wish someone had told me about income protection years ago. It would have cost me less than my gym membership.". In Emma's situation after not being able to return to work after an initial period of time (3 months in Emma's case), the income protection policy would have started paying her a monthly income replacement until she was able to return to work again. Whilst her emergency fund would still have been depleted and require re-building again in the future, she wouldn't also be trying to pay off credit card debt too if she had income protection in place.

Level 4: Additional Protection

Here's where you add extras based on your needs – critical illness cover, private medical insurance, legal expenses cover, even pet insurance.

QUICK CHECK-IN: Which level of protection do you feel least confident about right now?

Getting the Balance Right

There's a sweet spot with insurance: enough to genuinely protect you, but not so much you're paying for cover you can't actually use.

Over-insuring can happen if, for example, you take out multiple income protection policies thinking they'll all pay out together. They won't, there are usually maximum claim limits.

Under-insuring is the other trap. You take out cover but forget to update it when your circumstances change, perhaps you've moved house, taken on a bigger mortgage, or your cost of living has increased.

It is not unusual to find life insurance which was taken out with a very first house purchase (pre-children or additional responsibilities), but which hasn't been reviewed at all since. Multiple house moves later, mortgages often more than doubling from that initial purchase and several dependent children later, your life insurance need looks vastly different from those early days which means those original policies may no longer be fit for purpose.

Here are my golden rules for you to consider with your own situation:

- Check what you already get through your employer. You might have life cover, income protection, or private medical insurance without even realising.
- Review your cover once a year, ideally on the same date you do other financial admin.
- Factor in inflation – your cover amount might have been perfect five years ago, but the cost of living has moved on so is your cover still the right amount for your needs?
- Some insurance policies offer an indexation option which means that the cover will automatically increase every year to help keep pace with inflation, though you will likely need to select this option at the outset. Your annual premiums will also increase each year to meet the cost of the additional cover too.

Smart Shopping for Cover

If you're buying or renewing insurance:

- **Shop around.** Comparison sites are a great starting point, but remember to check what's actually covered – the cheapest policy isn't always the best value.
- **Check for cashback.** Sites like Quidco or TopCashback can give you a nice little bonus.
- **Negotiate.** You'd be amazed how often renewal quotes drop the moment you ask, "Is that your best price?"
- **Bundle if it makes sense.** Sometimes holding multiple policies with the same provider reduces fees.

Protecting Your Digital Financial Life

Our financial lives are increasingly digital, creating both opportunities and vulnerabilities that previous generations never faced. From cryptocurrency holdings to online-only investment platforms, digital assets require specialised protection strategies. But as our financial world moves online, so too do the risks. Increasingly, financial control and coercion can extend into the digital realm through the misuse of technology to monitor, restrict, or undermine someone's financial independence. This form of digital abuse might involve accessing online banking, tracking spending, intercepting communications, or even using smart devices to observe movements or activity. Protecting your digital footprint is therefore just as important as safeguarding your physical and financial assets.

Understanding Your Digital Asset Portfolio:

Start by cataloguing all your digital financial assets. This includes obvious items like cryptocurrency holdings, but also online-only bank accounts, digital investment platforms, automated savings apps, and even reward program balances that have monetary value.

Many women discover they have more digital assets than expected. That online savings account you opened for a specific goal, the investment app you tried last year, the cryptocurrency you bought out of curiosity, these scattered digital holdings can represent significant value and create security vulnerabilities if not properly managed.

Cryptocurrency and Digital Investment Security:

Cryptocurrency requires a different security approach than traditional investments. Unlike bank accounts that offer fraud protection and recovery options, cryptocurrency transactions are generally irreversible. This means the responsibility for security rests entirely with you.

Hardware wallets provide the highest security for significant cryptocurrency holdings, keeping your digital assets offline and protected from online threats. However, they require careful management of recovery seeds, those 12 or 24-word phrases that provide access to your holdings. These seeds should be stored securely and separately from the hardware wallet itself.

For smaller holdings or regular trading, reputable exchanges offer convenience with reasonable security, but remember you're trusting a third party with your assets. Diversifying across storage methods can balance security and accessibility.

Digital Estate Planning:

Your digital assets need specific estate planning attention because traditional inheritance laws weren't designed for them. Unlike physical assets or bank accounts, digital assets may become inaccessible without proper planning.

Create a secure digital asset inventory that includes account information, access methods, and storage locations. This document should be stored securely and updated regularly as your digital holdings change.

Consider appointing a technically competent digital executor, someone who understands cryptocurrency, online platforms, and digital security. This person may be different from your primary executor, and they'll need detailed instructions for accessing and managing your digital assets.

Regulatory Landscape Navigation:
The regulatory environment for digital assets continues evolving rapidly. Stay informed about tax obligations, reporting requirements, and regulatory changes that might affect your holdings. In the UK, cryptocurrency gains are subject to capital gains tax, and detailed record-keeping is essential for compliance.

Consider professional guidance for significant digital asset holdings, as tax optimisation strategies for traditional investments may not apply to digital assets.

DIGITAL ABUSE WARNING
Financial abusers often monitor:

- Bank account access and online banking
- Email and social media accounts
- Phone and internet usage
- GPS location through apps or car systems
- Smart home devices and security systems

If you suspect monitoring:

- Change passwords only from a safe device/location
- Enable two-factor authentication using a device your abuser cannot access
- Consider using banking and email from safe locations (library, work, friend's house)
- Be aware that new financial apps or accounts may trigger notifications to shared devices

Thinking Long-Term: Beyond the Emergencies

Protection also means preparing for the financial seasons you can see coming. That includes:

Pension Planning

Know what you're entitled to, where your pensions are, and how they're invested. Billions of pounds are sitting in "lost" pensions because people move jobs and never consolidate or track them.

Estate Planning

If you're not married and your partner dies without a will, you have no automatic claim to their estate. Even if you are married, inheritance rules might not work the way you think. Wills, powers of attorney, and named beneficiaries on pensions and policies are non-negotiables.

I frequently meet couples who have been together for decades but never married. They assume "common law" means they'd automatically inherit from each other, but it doesn't. Working through what would actually happen to each other's assets without any of these things in place is often a significant "oh no!" moment which then helps to spur on putting everything properly in place.

Note on Wills vs Beneficiaries

Your will doesn't always cover everything. Pensions, life insurance, and some savings accounts are passed on via beneficiary forms, not your will. Make sure both match your wishes.

More Than One Basket

Another protective strategy I am witnessing with increasing frequency and focus is multiple income streams. A side hustle, rental income, or investment income can help you weather storms and give you flexibility in the future. This doesn't mean you need to start three businesses tomorrow, it's about gradually creating options.

One of the most common questions I'm asked is "What's a good side hustle?" The truth is, there isn't a one-size-fits-all answer. A good side hustle is one that fits your skills, your available time, and, importantly, your energy. It should feel like an extension of your strengths rather than another drain on your already busy life. For one woman that might be turning a creative hobby into a small income stream; for another, it could be using professional skills for freelance work. What matters most is that it works for you and supports your bigger financial picture.

Chapter 8 Workbook Exercises: Securing Your Financial Future

1. **Quick Knowledge Check: I currently have:**
   - ☐ Life insurance
   - ☐ Income protection
   - ☐ Critical illness cover
   - ☐ None of these
   - ☐ Don't know

2. **One Key Reflection: My biggest protection concern is:**
   - ☐ What happens to my family if I can't work
   - ☐ How to pay bills if I'm ill
   - ☐ Protecting my assets
   - ☐ Understanding what I actually need

3. **Priority Action This Week:**
   - ☐ Review what protection I get through my employer
   - ☐ Calculate how much life cover I might need
   - ☐ Research one type of protection I don't currently have

Part 3: Growing Your Wealth

"I'm not going to limit myself just because people won't accept the fact that I can do something else." - Dolly Parton

With your financial foundations in place and the right protections to safeguard what matters most, you're ready to take the next step, moving from simply protecting your position to actively building it.

This part is about moving beyond "keeping afloat" into intentionally creating the life and future you want. We'll explore practical, confidence-building ways to invest, create multiple streams of income, and plan with purpose for the decades ahead. You'll discover how to align your investments with your values, make informed decisions without fear, and balance growth with security.

Growing your wealth isn't about chasing the next big win or taking unnecessary risks. It's about making deliberate, well-informed choices that reflect your goals, your timeframes, and your personal values, so that your money supports the life you want to live, now and in the future.

And where better to begin than with one of the most powerful tools for long-term financial freedom: investing.

Chapter 9:
Investment Fundamentals for Women

Over the years, I've noticed something fascinating. When the word "investing" comes up, most women I meet fall into one of two camps. The first feel as though they've been left out of the conversation entirely, like it's some closed-door club speaking a secret language they were never taught. The second group? They find the topic painfully dull… until we start talking about it in a different way.

And that's the thing. It's not that women inherently find investing boring or intimidating. It's that, too often, the conversation is wrapped in a suit-and-tie, male-scripted language that doesn't connect with our lived experiences or values. Shift the conversation to what the money is for – helping a friend's business grow, funding your child's future, or building a safety net that lets you step off the treadmill one day and the whole energy changes.

So, let's reframe investing. This is not a competitive sport. It's not a gamble. And it's definitely not about proving yourself against someone else's scoreboard. Investing is one of the most important tools we have for creating long-term financial freedom. Done intentionally, it's about planting seeds for your future self, your loved ones, and even the world you want to help shape.

LOSS AVERSION IN ACTION

The human brain feels the pain of a loss about twice as strongly as it feels the joy of a gain. This explains why investors panic-sell when markets dip, even though history shows markets recover. Knowing this bias exists can help you stay invested and avoid crystallising temporary losses.

Your Investment Personality

Traditional investing guides love to talk about "risk tolerance", whether you're aggressive, conservative, or somewhere in between. But I've found this misses the heart of the matter. I prefer to think about your investment personality.

This is the unique combination of your life circumstances, your personal values, and your goals.

Some women love to dive deep, researching every detail before committing to an investment. Others go more on instinct. They want to feel a connection with the businesses they support. And some are happy to understand the big picture but would rather delegate the day-to-day decisions to a trusted adviser.

Your investment personality is also shaped by your timeframe and purpose. Are you investing for something ten years away, like a child's education? Or is your goal further out; a "work-optional" lifestyle in your 50s? Knowing not just what you want but when you want it can guide your choices far more effectively than a vague label like "high risk" or "low risk."

Think of It Like a Garden

I love the analogy of your financial life as a garden. You wouldn't plant only one type of flower and expect it to bloom all year round. Instead, you'd have a mix, some that give vibrant colour quickly, some that take time to mature, and a few sturdy perennials that keep coming back.

In investing, that mix might look like:

- **Growth investments:** like shares in companies that can flourish over the long term but need patience and resilience through the ups and downs of the changing seasons along the way.
- **Income investments:** such as bonds or dividend-paying shares that provide a steadier "harvest" you can reinvest or spend as needed.
- **Cash:** your water reserve which doesn't grow much but is there to keep things alive in a dry spell.
- **Alternatives:** the unusual plants that make your garden unique, like property, private business investments, or other niche opportunities.

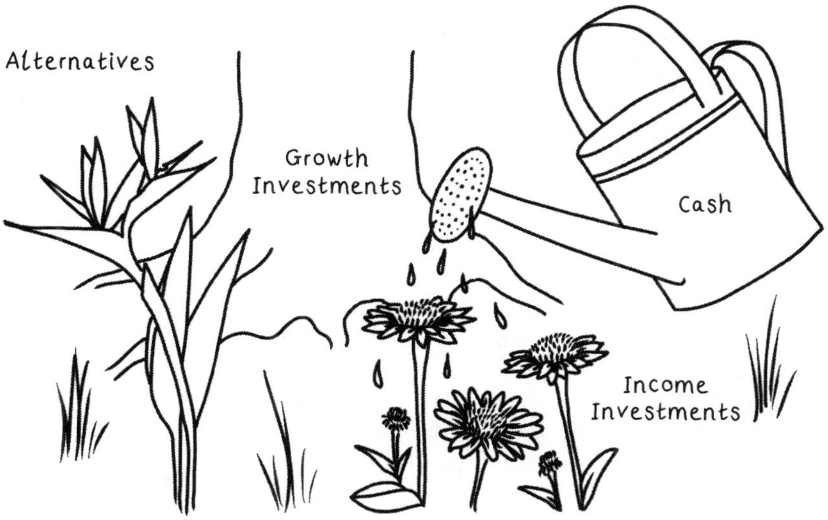

A healthy portfolio is like a well-tended garden: resilient to changing seasons, diverse enough to thrive in different conditions, and always reflective of the person who's growing it.

PAUSE HERE: Which part of your garden is flourishing? Which part feels neglected?

Why Cash is Not an Investment

Cash is essential. You need it for your emergency fund, your day-to-day spending, and those moments when life throws you a curveball. Cash gives you stability and quick access. But here's the tricky part: cash is not an investment.

It's a bit like keeping seeds in a drawer. They're safe (they won't blow away or get eaten by birds) but they also won't grow. In fact, over time, they lose potential.

With money, that "loss of potential" comes from inflation; the gradual rise in the cost of living. If inflation is 5% and your savings account pays you 2%, you're effectively losing 3% of your purchasing power each year. The number in your account might not change, but what it can buy quietly shrinks.

Holding too much cash for too long can give a false sense of security. Yes, it won't swing up and down like the stock market, but it also won't work hard for you. And if your goal is to grow wealth, you need some of your money out in the world, working (planting, sprouting, and bearing fruit).

Think of cash as the watering can for your financial garden, vital for survival in dry spells, but not the thing that produces the blooms. Too much water and no planting? You'll never see the flowers.

Why Shares Over Property (for Most Starting Out)

Property is familiar – we live in it, we see the "For Sale" boards, and the news loves to talk about house prices. There is a sense of security about being able to hold the key to the property we own. But property as an investment has downsides: it ties up large sums in a single asset, is expensive to buy and sell, isn't easily split if you need just part of the money and isn't always easy to sell at the time that you want (we refer to this type of investment as being illiquid).

Historically, property was an attractive investment option for some investors because of the ability to borrow money via a mortgage and therefore own a higher value investment from the outset. However, as legislation and regulation has changed over time, tax treatment of mortgage interest has become less attractive, borrowing criteria around mortgages have become tighter and the cost of owning property can be high.

Shares, on the other hand:

- **Are flexible** – you can start with small, regular amounts.
- **Offer instant diversification** – you can own hundreds of companies worldwide in one fund.
- **Are liquid** – this means you can sell them quickly if needed.
- **Have historically outperformed** – over long periods, global shares have beaten both property and cash.

That doesn't mean property has no place, but for most women building wealth from scratch, shares are the more accessible and scalable starting point.

What Is Pound-Cost Averaging?

One of the simplest but most powerful investment strategies is something called pound-cost averaging. Don't be put off by the jargon, the concept is actually very straightforward.

Instead of trying to guess the "perfect time" to invest (which even professionals struggle with), pound-cost averaging means investing a fixed amount of money regularly, say £100 or £500 each month, regardless of whether the market is up or down.

Over time, this smooths out the highs and lows of market movements because:

- When prices are high, your fixed amount buys fewer shares or units.
- When prices are low, that same fixed amount buys more shares or units.

This consistency helps reduce the emotional stress of wondering *"Am I buying at the wrong time?"* and avoids the risk of keeping money sitting in cash because you're waiting for the "perfect" moment to invest.

A Simple Example

Imagine you invest £200 each month into a fund:

- **Month 1:** Price per unit is £10 → you buy 20 units
- **Month 2:** Price drops to £5 → you buy 40 units
- **Month 3:** Price rises to £8 → you buy 25 units

After 3 months, you've invested £600 in total and own 85 units. Your average cost per unit is about £7.06. Even though the price went up and down, you didn't need to time the market, you simply bought consistently, and your average worked itself out.

Why Women in Particular Benefit

For women, who often juggle irregular income, career breaks, and long-term goals, pound-cost averaging can be especially effective:

- It builds investing into your routine like a direct debit, so it happens automatically (no procrastination required).
- It makes market ups and downs less intimidating , dips become opportunities rather than disasters.
- It aligns with long-term investing, which is where women already have a natural advantage because of our longer life expectancy.

Things to Remember:

- Pound-cost averaging doesn't guarantee profits, if the market keeps falling over a long period, you could still lose money.
- If you happen to receive a large lump sum (inheritance, bonus, business exit), sometimes investing it straight away works out better historically. But for most day-to-day investing, a regular plan is an accessible and stress-free approach.

QUICK CHECK-IN: If you set up an automatic monthly investment right now, how much could you comfortably commit? Even £50 a month can make a significant difference over decades.

How to Get Started

Step 1: Choose Your "Wrapper"

This is the container your investments sit in:

- ISA (Stocks & Shares ISA): will offer you tax-free growth and income.
- Pension (SIPP or workplace): provides tax relief on contributions, but is then locked away until later life.
- General Investment Account (GIA): flexible to top up and withdraw, but any income and capital gains can be taxed (typically the wrapper of choice once the ISA wrapper has been fully utilised).

Step 2: Pick Your Approach

- Passive Funds: (index funds/ETFs) track the market; low-cost and hands-off.
- Active Funds: run by fund managers trying to outperform; higher cost and no guarantees.
- Multi-Asset Funds: ready-made blends of shares, bonds, and more, great for beginners.

Step 3: Start Small and Regular

Set up a monthly direct debit to drip-feed money in – pound-cost averaging smooths out the bumps.

Research Without Overwhelm

Decide the mix: your "asset allocation" between shares, bonds, cash, etc.

Pick the broad market: e.g., global shares, UK shares, emerging markets.

Select the fund: low-cost, well-established, with a clear strategy.
Here's a good rule to follow: if you can't explain what you own and why in one sentence, it's too complex for now.

Understanding Risk, Volatility and Time

Here are some important concepts to consider:

Risk in investing is simply the range of possible outcomes. That means when you invest, there's a spectrum of what could happen, from your investment growing in value, to it staying the same, to it falling (sometimes sharply, at least for a while). Risk isn't just about the chance of losing money; it's about the level of uncertainty around what your returns might be. A savings account has low risk because the range of outcomes is tiny, you know almost exactly what interest you'll earn. Shares, on the other hand, have a much wider range of possible outcomes. They could grow significantly over time, but they can also drop in value along the way.

Volatility is the up-and-down movement in value. In practice, this means that the price of an investment rarely moves in a straight line. It can rise one day, fall the next, and sometimes swing quite dramatically in a short space of time. These fluctuations are a normal part of investing – they reflect changes in the economy, company performance, investor confidence, even world events. Volatility doesn't necessarily mean something is "bad" or "unsafe"; it's simply the visible movement of markets as they react to new information. While it can feel unsettling, especially if you check your account daily, don't forget that over longer periods those ups and downs tend to smooth out and the overall direction has historically been upward.

In the short term, shares can fall sharply. But over longer periods, the chance of ending up with more than you started rises dramatically.

Think of investing like hiking up a mountain. The path isn't a straight, smooth incline, there are rocky patches, steep climbs, and moments when you dip down before heading up again. If you focus only on the bumps under your feet, it can feel exhausting. But if you keep your eyes on the summit and remember why you started, those ups and downs become just part of the journey to the view you've been working towards.

Match your investments to your timeframe:

- **0–3 years** – keep it in cash.
- **3–7 year**s – balanced mix of shares and bonds.
- **7+ years** – lean more on shares for growth.

Time isn't just a healer, it's a risk-reducer. The longer your money stays invested, the less impact short-term swings tend to have.

NOTE ON RISK AND RETURN: Higher potential returns usually mean higher risk. That doesn't mean avoiding risk altogether, but finding the balance that matches your goals and timeframes.

Making Sense of the Markets

Investment markets can seem intimidating, especially when the headlines scream about crashes or booms. But strip away the jargon, and a "market" is simply a place where people buy and sell things – in this case, investments. And here's the secret: markets are not cold, rational machines. They're reflections of human behaviour, our fears, hopes, and sometimes our impatience.

At the heart of any market lies trust. We assign value to an investment not because of some universal truth carved in stone, but because enough people believe in that value at the same time. Think of money itself: a £20 note is just paper and ink. Its "worth" comes from the shared agreement, the collective trust, that others will accept it in exchange for goods or services. The same principle applies to investments. Shares in a company are valuable because investors trust that the company will continue to create products, serve customers, and generate profits in the future. When that trust grows, prices rise. When that trust wavers, prices fall.

This human element means markets often move less on hard facts and more on perception. A rumour, a news headline, or even a collective mood can shift billions of pounds in minutes. Understanding this makes investing less mysterious. You're not battling an impersonal machine, you're navigating a system driven by human trust, behaviour, and belief. And while human behaviour can be unpredictable in the short term, over the long term trust tends to reward businesses and investments that deliver real value.

Think of it like a new restaurant in town. On opening night, a few people go and tell their friends it's brilliant. Soon it's fully booked every evening, not because everyone has eaten there, but because they trust the opinions of others. The same thing can happen in reverse; a couple of bad reviews and suddenly the bookings dry up. Investment markets work much the same way: confidence and trust can build momentum quickly, and evaporate just as fast.

Another way to picture it is like the changing seasons. Markets move in cycles – prices rise and fall. Sometimes the garden enjoys a rainy spring where everything grows quickly. Sometimes there's a harsh frost that knocks things back. The danger comes when we react emotionally: pulling out perfectly healthy plants (selling investments) during the frost, or planting too much in a frenzy during the sunny spell.

One of the most powerful things you can do as an investor is to learn the difference between noise (short-term chatter that makes headlines) and signals (meaningful shifts worth paying attention to). This skill grows with time, experience, and the willingness to pause before making big decisions.

Finding Your First Step

Starting to invest doesn't require a huge sum of money or encyclopaedic knowledge. What matters most is creating the habit. That might mean beginning with your workplace pension, opening an ISA, or setting up a small monthly investment into a diversified fund.

If the thought of investing still feels overwhelming, lean into community and conversation. Many women I've spoken to have built confidence through small investment groups, mentoring relationships, or simply by making investing a topic they're willing to discuss openly with friends.

Technology has also made it easier than ever, from hands-on platforms where you choose every investment, to simple "set-and-forget" apps that automatically diversify for you.

Overcoming the Barriers

In my conversations with the women that I've worked with, its been clear to me that women often face unique barriers to investment that I believe deserve calling out. Research consistently shows a confidence gap in financial decision-making, not because women lack capability, but because societal messages have often discouraged financial engagement. Recognising these patterns is the first step to moving beyond them.

Career interruptions for caregiving responsibilities can also impact investment trajectories. Rather than viewing these as setbacks, we can develop strategies that accommodate life's natural ebbs and flows. This might mean more aggressive investment during high-earning periods or creative approaches during caregiving years.

Building support networks specifically for investment knowledge helps counteract the historical exclusion of women from financial conversations. Whether through formal investment clubs, informal gatherings, or professional associations, connecting with others on similar journeys provides both practical knowledge and emotional reinforcement.

Perhaps most importantly, recognising and challenging internalised limiting beliefs about money and investing opens new possibilities. Many women have absorbed subtle messages about their capacity for financial growth. Identifying these beliefs, often expressed in phrases like "I'm just not good with numbers" or "investing is too complicated", creates space for new, empowering narratives about your financial capabilities.

Understanding Investment Approaches Through Your Money Personality

Your money personality influences how you naturally approach investing – but your timeframe and specific goals should ultimately guide your strategy. A 25-year-old with 40 years until retirement can typically afford more risk than a 55-year-old planning to retire in a decade, regardless of personality type.

This section isn't investment advice or a recommendation. Instead, it's designed to help you understand:

- Which investment approaches might feel more comfortable based on your personality
- What behavioural patterns to be aware of
- How to have more productive conversations with a financial adviser

Always speak with a qualified financial planner who can assess your complete situation, including your timeframe, goals, risk capacity, and personal circumstances.

Status Seekers: The Achievement Approach

Natural Tendencies: you're likely drawn to investments that feel impressive, trackable, and competitive. You may enjoy researching individual stocks, watching portfolio performance, and having sophisticated-sounding investments to discuss.

TIME HORIZON CONSIDERATIONS

Long timeframe (20+ years to goal):

- You have time to recover from market volatility, so higher-risk growth investments may be appropriate
- Consider how achievement milestones (first £10k, £50k, £100k invested) can keep you motivated through market downturns
- Your competitive nature could work for you here – compete with your past self, not with day traders

Medium timeframe (10–20 years):

- Balance your desire for growth with increasing need for stability as your goal approaches
- Your tendency to track performance closely can be useful for regular rebalancing
- Focus on consistent accumulation rather than trying to time the market

Short timeframe (under 10 years):

- Your personality may push you toward riskier investments to "make up time," but this can backfire
- Consider how achieving your goal on schedule matters more than achieving it spectacularly
- Your competitive drive might be better directed toward maximising contributions rather than chasing returns

Behavioural Strengths to Leverage:

- Your motivation to track and measure progress
- Willingness to learn and research investments
- Comfort with taking calculated risks
- Goal-oriented mindset

Behavioural Risks to Watch:

- Over-trading to beat benchmarks or peers
- Concentrating too much in individual stocks or "impressive" investments
- Letting ego drive decisions (investing in things you don't understand because they sound sophisticated)
- Comparing your returns to others without considering different risk levels or timeframes

Conversation Starters for Your Financial Adviser:

- "Given my timeframe of [X years], what level of risk is actually appropriate for me?"
- "How do I balance my desire for growth with the reality of my timeline?"
- "What benchmarks should I actually be measuring myself against?"

Guardians: The Security-First Approach

Natural Tendencies: you prioritise safety and predictability. You're likely drawn to familiar, regulated products and may feel anxious about market volatility. You probably research extensively before making decisions and prefer gradual changes.

TIME HORIZON CONSIDERATIONS

Long timeframe (20+ years to goal):

- Ironically, playing it "too safe" with only cash and bonds may be the riskiest strategy due to inflation
- You have decades to ride out market volatility – short-term drops won't matter
- Your careful, steady approach is actually ideal for long-term investing if you can overcome initial hesitation
- Consider how inflation erodes "safe" money over 20–30 years

Medium timeframe (10–20 years):

- Your cautious nature is more appropriate here – some protection becomes important
- Gradual shifts toward stability as your goal approaches align with your personality
- Your tendency to research thoroughly can help you understand why some volatility is still acceptable

Short timeframe (under 10 years):

- Your instinct for security is well-matched to your timeline
- Focus on capital preservation rather than growth
- Your risk-averse nature protects you from making desperate, high-risk moves

Behavioural Strengths to Leverage:

- Consistency and discipline with regular contributions
- Thorough research and understanding before committing
- Unlikely to panic-sell or make impulsive decisions
- Patient, long-term perspective

Behavioural Risks to Watch:

- Paralysis by analysis – researching forever without taking action
- Holding too much in cash/low-return products, losing to inflation
- Letting fear of short-term losses prevent long-term growth
- Misunderstanding what "safe" actually means over different timeframes

Conversation Starters for Your Financial Adviser:

- "Given my [X year] timeframe, what's the actual risk of market-based investments?"
- "Can you show me historical data on recovery times after market downturns?"
- "How do I balance my need for security with the risk of inflation?"
- "What would a gradual approach to increasing risk look like for someone like me?"

Free Spirits: The Values-Aligned Approach

Natural Tendencies: you want your investments to reflect your values and support causes you care about. You're drawn to ESG (Environmental, Social, Governance) funds, impact investing, and companies whose mission resonates with you. However, you may struggle with consistency and detailed financial management.

TIME HORIZON CONSIDERATIONS

Long timeframe (20+ years to goal):

- Perfect opportunity to align values and growth – you have time for impact investments to mature
- Your passion for causes can sustain motivation through market volatility
- Automatic systems are crucial because your attention may wander over decades
- Long-term thematic investing (climate, social justice) suits both your values and timeline

Medium timeframe (10–20 years):

- Continue values alignment but ensure adequate diversification
- Your enthusiasm for specific causes shouldn't override practical diversification needs
- Automation becomes even more critical as you approach your goal
- Balance impact focus with ensuring you'll actually reach your financial target

Short timeframe (under 10 years):

- Values still matter, but goal achievement takes priority
- Don't sacrifice necessary stability for perfect values alignment
- Your tendency toward sporadic attention is most dangerous here – automation is essential
- Focus on well-established ESG funds rather than experimental impact investments

Behavioural Strengths to Leverage:

- Emotional connection to your investments keeps you engaged
- Willingness to learn about new approaches and ideas
- Long-term thematic thinking (climate change isn't a short-term issue)
- Comfort with unconventional approaches

Behavioural Risks to Watch:

- Sporadic attention leading to neglected accounts or missed opportunities
- Over-concentrating in specific causes at the expense of diversification
- Making emotional decisions based on single news stories
- Neglecting "boring but necessary" foundations (emergency funds, pensions)

Conversation Starters for Your Financial Adviser:

- "How can I align my investments with my values without sacrificing diversification?"
- "What's the performance track record of ESG funds compared to traditional funds?"
- "How do I set up automation so my values-based investments grow even when I'm not paying attention?"
- "Given my [X year] timeline, how much can I prioritise impact over returns?"

Avoiders: The Simple Automation Approach

Natural Tendencies: financial decisions trigger anxiety or overwhelm, so you avoid them. You may have analysis paralysis, fear of making mistakes, or simply find finance boring and confusing. You need simplicity above all else.

TIME HORIZON CONSIDERATIONS

Long timeframe (20+ years to goal):

- Your best friend: automation and "set it and forget it" approaches
- Target-date funds are literally designed for people like you – they adjust automatically as you age
- Your tendency to avoid checking accounts constantly is actually an advantage for long-term investing
- The longer your timeframe, the more you can benefit from simple, automated growth

Medium timeframe (10–20 years):

- Simple, automated systems remain crucial
- You'll need slightly more check-ins as you approach your goal, but still minimal
- Your avoidance of constant monitoring protects you from panic-selling
- Focus on one or two funds maximum – complexity is your enemy

Short timeframe (under 10 years):

- Simplicity becomes even more important – you can't afford analysis paralysis
- Your timeline means you need some structure and oversight, even if uncomfortable
- Consider if this is where professional management becomes worth the cost
- Automation protects you from procrastination at a critical time

Behavioural Strengths to Leverage:

- Once set up, you're unlikely to over-trade or panic-sell
- Not constantly checking means you avoid emotional reactions to volatility
- Simplicity preference prevents you from over-complicating things
- Automation suits your hands-off preference

Behavioural Risks to Watch:

- Never starting due to overwhelm or perfectionism
- Neglecting accounts entirely, missing important deadlines or opportunities
- Panic-selling during downturns because you haven't stayed educated
- Analysis paralysis preventing even simple first steps

Conversation Starters for Your Financial Adviser:

- "I find financial decisions overwhelming – what's the simplest possible approach given my [X year] timeframe?"
- "Can you recommend one or two funds that require minimal decision-making?"
- "How often do I actually need to review my investments?"
- "What's the minimum I need to understand to make this work?"

ACTION STEP: Matching Personality to Timeline

Before speaking with a financial adviser, consider:

1. **Your timeframe:** How many years until you need this money?
   - 20+ years = Long-term
   - 10–20 years = Medium-term
   - Under 10 years = Short-term

2. **Your personality strengths:** What natural tendencies can you leverage?

3. **Your personality risks:** What behavioural patterns might sabotage you?

4. **Your automation needs:** How much do you need systems to protect you from yourself?

Regardless of your archetype:

- Start investing as early as possible (time is your greatest asset)
- Diversify across different asset classes and geographies
- Keep costs low (choose index funds over actively managed when possible)
- Stay consistent with regular investments
- Don't try to time the market
- Focus on your long-term goals, not short-term market movements

A financial planner can help you design an investment strategy that works with your personality and timeframe, not against them. The goal isn't to change who you are, it's to build a system that succeeds because of who you are.

The Gentle Truth

Investing is not about being fearless. It's about being intentional. It's about accepting that there will be moments of doubt, that not every choice will be perfect, and that you can still create a beautiful, thriving financial garden over time.

So release any guilt for "starting late" or "not knowing enough." You know enough to begin. And every step you take from here will be a gift to your future self.

Chapter 9 Workbook Exercises: Investment Fundamentals

1. **Quick Knowledge Check:** For long-term wealth building, which is typically most important?
   - ☐ Perfect market timing
   - ☐ Picking winning stocks
   - ☐ Time in market
   - ☐ Avoiding all losses

2. **One Key Reflection:**
   My biggest investment barrier is:
   - ☐ Don't know where to start
   - ☐ Fear of losing money
   - ☐ Too complex
   - ☐ Not enough money
   - ☐ Don't trust the system

3. **Priority Action This Week:**
   - ☐ Research one investment platform suitable for beginners
   - ☐ Calculate how much I could invest monthly
   - ☐ Read one article about long-term investing

Chapter 10:
Sustainable and Ethical Investing

Women have always been leaders when it comes to making money decisions that align with values. Whether it's choosing where to shop, what brands to support, or how to spend household income, we often look beyond the price tag and ask, "Does this fit with what I believe in?" Sustainable investing is simply extending that same instinct into how you grow your wealth.

What ESG Really Means (and Why It Matters to You)

ESG is a term which is now widely used. In case you've not come across it before or you are unsure what it means, it stands for Environmental Social Governance.

Environmental, Social, and Governance – three lenses for looking at a company beyond just its profits.

Think of it like choosing a school for your child, or an employer you might want to work for.

- **Environmental:** Does the school have a green space, care about sustainability, avoid waste?
- **Social:** How does it treat pupils and staff? Is it inclusive and supportive?
- **Governance:** Is it well-run, transparent, and accountable?

Those same questions apply to companies, they just look bigger in scale. Sustainable investing has evolved dramatically from its origins in simple exclusionary screening, avoiding "sin stocks" like tobacco or firearms. Today's approach encompasses a sophisticated understanding of how environmental, social, and governance factors impact both company performance and global wellbeing.

Environmental: considerations extend beyond basic compliance to how companies address climate change, resource usage, pollution, and biodiversity. Forward-thinking businesses now recognise that environmental stewardship isn't just ethical, it's essential for long-term viability in a resource-constrained world.

Social: social factors examine how companies manage relationships with employees, suppliers, customers, and communities. Issues like workplace safety, diversity and inclusion, labour standards, and community engagement fall within this category. Companies that excel in these areas often benefit from stronger customer loyalty, employee retention, and social license to operate.

Governance: addresses the internal systems directing and controlling a company. Board diversity, executive compensation, shareholder rights, and business ethics all influence how well a company serves all stakeholders. Strong governance typically correlates with better long-term decision-making and fewer damaging controversies.

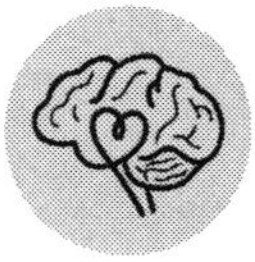

WHY VALUES MATTER

When investments align with our values, the brain's reward system (dopamine pathways) is more engaged. This makes it easier to stay committed for the long term. It's not "soft" to align money with values, it's neuroscience-backed staying power.

Myth Busting: Do Values Mean Lower Returns?

For years, it was understood that if you invested with your values, you'd have to sacrifice returns. Today, investing in the ESG space has dramatically changed and research increasingly shows the opposite is in fact often true; companies with strong ESG practices often do better over the long term because they avoid scandals, manage risks better, and attract loyal customers and talented staff.

Finding Your Values Compass

Before you invest sustainably, ask yourself:

- What issues matter most to me? Climate change? Gender equality? Community development?
- Where would I feel uncomfortable making a profit? For example, tobacco, weapons, or exploitative labour.

Translating values into concrete investment criteria requires thoughtfulness. If environmental sustainability matters most to you, you might focus on companies leading in renewable energy or circular economy practices. If gender equality is your priority, you might seek companies with strong representation of women in leadership and equitable policies. You might discover a hierarchy which then becomes your "values compass" for choosing investments.

Often, values exist in tension with each other. A company might excel in environmental initiatives but struggle with workplace diversity. Another might have exemplary human rights practices but governance concerns. Recognising these complexities allows you to make nuanced decisions about which trade-offs align with your hierarchy of values.

Creating a personal ethical investment statement can bring clarity to this process. This isn't a rigid document but rather an evolving expression of what matters most to you and how you hope your investments will contribute to positive change. Revisiting this statement annually helps ensure your investments remain aligned with your evolving values.

PAUSE HERE: Create your own short Ethical Investment Statement. Here's an example: "I invest in companies that respect the planet, treat people fairly, and operate with integrity. I will not invest in industries that cause harm to healthor the environment." It doesn't have to be perfect; it just givesyou a reference point.

Ways to Put Your Values into Action

There's no single "right" way to invest ethically, so here are some common approaches that you might want to consider:

1. **ESG-Integrated Funds**
   - Investment funds that filter companies based on ESG criteria alongside traditional performance analysis.
   - Great for beginners because professionals do the screening for you.

   Example: Lucy discovered her workplace pension was invested in several fossil fuel companies. She'd never thought to ask, it was just "defaulted" when she joined the company. After a quick call to her pension provider, she switched to a sustainable fund option focused on renewable energy, green tech, and companies with strong ESG ratings.

   "It took less than 15 minutes to change, but it felt huge knowing my future is being funded by businesses I actually believe in."

2. **Impact Investing**
   Actively seeking companies whose core mission solves a problem like renewable energy providers, affordable housing developers, or healthcare innovators.

3. **Community shares, credit unions, and FCA-authorised community investment funds**
   Directing money into projects that benefit local economies or underserved areas such as community banks or small business funds.

4. **Shareholder Advocacy**
   Owning shares gives you a voice – even small investors can vote on company policies.

   Example: Melissa works in HR and is passionate about workplace equality. She started buying small amounts of stock in companies she admired for their mission, but also in those she thought could improve. Through shareholder voting, she backed resolutions on pay transparency, maternity policies, and board diversity.

Avoiding the Greenwashing Trap

Not every "eco-friendly" or "socially responsible" label is what it seems. Some companies talk the talk without walking the walk.

Look for:

Independent ratings (e.g., MSCI, Sustainalytics): These are like the nutrition labels of the investing world. They give you an objective view of whether a company is genuinely making progress on sustainability or just spinning a clever marketing story.

MSCI ESG Ratings: MSCI is one of the largest global providers of environmental, social, and governance (ESG) data. They grade companies on how well they manage issues such as climate change, labour rights, and corporate governance. A higher MSCI ESG rating means the company is managing these challenges better than its peers.

Sustainalytics: This research firm (part of Morningstar) looks at how exposed companies are to ESG-related risks and how effectively they're managing them. A lower "risk rating" suggests the business is less likely to face problems like environmental fines, lawsuits, or reputational scandals in the future.

Why this matters: ESG ratings help cut through the noise. They won't give you a perfect answer, but they do provide a clearer, independent view that can guide your choices. For investors, they're also a way of managing risk – companies with poor ESG practices are more likely to stumble in the long run. Look for:

- Transparent sustainability reports with measurable goals
- Evidence of progress, not just promises

If a company claims to be "carbon neutral" but doesn't disclose how, treat it like a diet pill with no ingredient list – proceed with caution!

NOTE ON ESG RATINGS: ESG stands for Environmental, Social, and Governance. Independent ratings from providers like MSCI or Sustainalytics score companies on these factors helping you look beyond glossy marketing.

Getting Started – Without Overwhelm

1. **Start with a small percentage** of your portfolio, perhaps 10–20% in ESG funds, and grow as you learn.
2. **Ask your pension provider** if they offer sustainable fund options (many do now).
3. **Work with an adviser** who understands sustainable investing and will align recommendations to your personal values.

Your Next Step

Sustainable investing is not about perfection, it's about progress. Even small shifts in where you put your money can have a ripple effect. The key is knowing what matters to you and taking intentional steps to align your investments.

Remember: Every pound you invest can be a vote for the kind of world you want to live in.

Chapter 10 Workbook Exercises: Sustainable And Ethical Investing

1. **Quick Knowledge Check:** ESG stands for:

    - E ______________________
    - S ______________________
    - G ______________________

2. **One Key Reflection:** When investing, the values most important to me are:

    ☐ Environmental protection
    ☐ Social equality
    ☐ Ethical business practices
    ☐ All of the above
    ☐ Financial returns are my priority

3. **Priority Action This Week:**

    ☐ Research what ESG funds my pension offers
    ☐ Check if my current investments align with my values
    ☐ Read about one sustainable investing approach

Chapter 11:
Property and Alternative Investments

When most people think about investing, their minds go straight to the stock market. But beyond shares and funds lies a whole other world, one filled with bricks and mortar, fine art, even digital currencies. These are what we call tangible and alternative investments, and they can play an exciting role in a diversified wealth-building strategy.

This chapter will walk you through some of the options, the realities behind them, and the questions you should be asking yourself before diving in.

Property as a Wealth-Building Path

For many women I work with, property is one of their largest and most familiar investments, even if they don't think of it that way. Your home is more than numbers on a spreadsheet; it's the place you live your life.
But for most people, it also becomes a major part of their wealth over time. Understanding that dual role is essential when making housing decisions.

The reality of investment properties differs substantially from the glamorised version often portrayed in media. Successful property investors approach real estate methodically, understanding local markets, tenant needs, ongoing maintenance requirements, and the true costs of ownership beyond the purchase price. Property investing requires active engagement rather than passive income, particularly in the early years.

How you approach property investing often depends on your life stage.

- In your 20s or 30s, you might buy a flat as your first home and later turn it into a rental.
- In mid-life, you might release equity from your main home to buy an investment property.
- Later still, you might look at commercial property or even small development projects.

Whatever your stage, the most successful investors tend to grow slowly and steadily, consolidating one purchase before leaping into the next. It's less "property empire overnight" and more "measured, long-term growth." This measured approach reduces risk while building long-term wealth.

PROPERTY OWNERSHIP & TAXATION TIMELINE (UK)

1963

INTRODUCTION OF CAPITAL GAINS TAX (CGT)
Tax introduced on profits from selling assets, including property (other than your main residence).

1974

RENT ACT
Tight rent controls and strong tenant protections - later relaxed to encourage private landlords.

1996

ASSURED SHORTHOLD TENANCY (AST)
Became the default rental agreement in England and Wales, shaping today's buy-to-let market.

2000

STAMP DUTY LAND TAX (SDLT) REFORM
Rates restructured - SDLT became a significant upfront cost for property buyers.

2003

BUY-TO-LET BOOM
Lenders expanded mortgage options, fuelling rapid growth of the private rental sector.

2013

ANNUAL TAX ON ENVELOPED DWELLINGS (ATED)
Introduced to discourage property ownership via companies to avoid tax.

2016

3% SDLT SURCHARGE
Additional tax on second homes and buy-to-let properties, reducing investor demand.

2017-2020

MORTGAGE INTEREST RELIEF RESTRICTION (SECTION 24)
Phased changes meant landlords could no longer fully deduct mortgage interest from rental income - replaced by a 20% tax credit.

2021

CGT REPORTING CHANGES
Property sellers required to report and pay CGT on UK residential property within 60 days of sale.

ONGOING

INHERITANCE TAX (IHT) RULES
Main Residence Nil-Rate Band gradually increased (introduced 2017), reducing IHT on family homes passed to direct descendants.

Thinking about your exit strategy

One point I rarely see discussed, and yet it is critical, is how you'll get out of a property investment when the time comes. Many owners focus on the buying stage, but very few think carefully about the selling stage until they're forced to. And that's when problems can arise.

Property has been a favoured investment asset over the years for many clients that I have worked with. The property landscape has changed over time – as mentioned in an earlier chapter, tax treatment for one has become less favourable and so it is always important to consider all the different aspects of a property purchase. However, perhaps even more importantly I want to highlight the point of exit from a property. In my experience this is rarely thought through in detail until it is often too late to plan well.

Let's consider these 2 points; releasing capital and potential taxation.

Properties that have been acquired early on in life may grow in value quite significantly over the years. Fast forward to a point in time where you are wanting to 'retire' (I say that here in a very loose sense because the word 'retire' I think needs unpacking further, which we will do in a later chapter). It may be that you need more income than the rental income is providing. Unless you have bought the property to pass on as part of an inheritance strategy, then there is likely going to be no benefit to you taking the property to your grave. This means you need to sell the property so you can access the value that is all locked up in it. But selling a property quickly to release cash is often far easier said than done.

I was working with a couple recently who owned a second home which they had enjoyed as their seaside bolt hole whilst their family were young. Now the children had all left home and the couple were considering their retirement. We identified that the property no longer formed part of their future. They could look to rent it out, but the hassle of finding tenants and maintaining a large property wasn't appealing. They also wanted a higher income than the rental income would generate. So, the plan developed into a strategy where they would sell the property and use the sale proceeds to then repay their mortgage on their main home, reducing their monthly outgoings, and also provide a lump sum to invest in order to generate their desired level of income. However, it took over a year for the property to sell. During this period of time their mortgage rate increased so their costs went up, they had no tenant in the property because they needed it to be empty whilst they were trying to sell it. They were generating no income, but still had high costs, and they had to draw down on their other liquid investments to fund their income needs. Not only did this mean rejigging their financial plan, it also meant selling investments at a time that wasn't ideal. And on top of these practical implications, it also meant a lot of stress and anxiety.

Much of this could have been avoided if it had been thought through with plenty of time to plan and make sure consideration was made for selling the property earlier on in their retirement planning, so that funds were available when needed.

I worked with a client, Margaret, who needed to release £100,000 from her buy-to-let portfolio to supplement her retirement income. She assumed she could sell within three months. Eight months later, after reducing the price twice, dealing with a survey issue, and having one buyer pull out, she finally completed the sale. By then, she'd taken on short-term debt to cover her living costs.

Historically property has been great for long-term wealth building. However, it is becoming far less attractive than it used to be and importantly, it's illiquid. This means you may not be able to sell it when you want to (or for how much you would like to). So it is important to think about your exit strategy. This should include:

- Realistic timescales: Budget 6–12 months for a sale in normal market conditions
- Tax planning: Capital Gains Tax can take a significant bite. Calculate this well in advance
- Alternative options: Could you remortgage instead of selling? Release equity rather than disposing of the asset?
- Professional advice: Speak to a financial planner AND a tax advisor before you need to sell

The best time to plan your property exit is when you're buying the property, not when you desperately need the cash.

NOTE ON PROPERTY SALES: Your main home is exempt from Capital Gains Tax. But second homes, holiday lets, or buy-to-lets may face a tax bill on gains when you sell.

The Rental Property Journey

Finding your entry point into property investing often begins with identifying markets you understand, where property prices and rental demand create viable investment opportunities. Sometimes this means investing in familiar neighbourhoods; other times, it might mean researching emerging areas with growth potential.

Understanding the full cycle of property ownership illuminates both the opportunities and responsibilities. From initial property selection and financing through tenant management, maintenance, eventual sale, and tax implications, each phase requires different skills and considerations.

Successful property investors develop systems for handling each phase effectively.

Building a reliable support team transforms property ownership from overwhelming to manageable. This team typically includes a knowledgeable real estate agent, responsive maintenance professionals, possibly a property manager, an accountant familiar with property taxation, and legal support for lease agreements. With the right team, even busy professionals can successfully incorporate property into their investment portfolios.

Balancing effort, return, and personal bandwidth prevents property investing from overwhelming other priorities. Some women discover they enjoy the hands-on aspects of property management, while others prefer more passive approaches through property managers or real estate investment trusts. Neither approach is inherently superior, the best strategy aligns with your interests, skills, and available time.

Beyond Traditional Real Estate

If you like the idea of property but not the hands-on side, you have options.

Real Estate Investment Trusts (REITs): These let you buy shares in companies that own or finance income-producing property, from flats and offices to shopping centres. They're traded like shares, so you get liquidity and professional management without dealing with tenants.

Crowdfunded real estate: These platforms pool investors' money to buy or develop property. They make it possible to get involved with smaller sums, though liquidity and transparency vary widely, so research is essential.

Commercial property: Often higher yields and longer leases than residential property, but also more specialist knowledge and sensitivity to economic cycles.

International property: Spreads your investment risk across countries, but brings extra complexity in legal systems, tax, currency exchange, and local management.

Exploring Other Alternatives

Alternative investments go beyond property and can be anything from antiques to angel investing. Each type of alternative is very different from the next and so although we lump them all under the classification "alternatives", each really requires their own attention. However, here are a few examples:

Collectibles: Art, antiques, vintage cars, memorabilia. For most people, this starts as a passion project, profit is the bonus. Success comes from deep expertise and patience.

My father collects Dinky Models. These are toy cars which he used to play with as a child and loved. His expertise is exceptional in these models – he knows how much a model is worth, whether there are any imperfections that could reduce the valuation and he can also spot the most convincing of fakes. But this expertise is primarily a passion. It has consumed hours of his time over the years and whilst he can turn his trading into an investment, his primary driver is his love of each model (and once you take the time he has spent over his lifetime the concept of profitability becomes questionable!).

Commodities: Precious metals, agricultural products, natural resources. Often used to hedge against inflation, but prices can swing dramatically.

Private equity and business investments: Backing companies that aren't listed on the stock exchange. These range from formal private equity funds investing in established private companies to angel investing in early-stage ventures. The common thread is potential for higher returns accompanied by higher risk and reduced liquidity compared to public markets.

This can often take the form of a friend who is starting a business and looking for an injection of cash to help them get going. If you are considering this then the actual structure of the investment into the company is important, as well as considering the risk of the investment and whether you are likely to receive your investment back or not.

Cryptocurrency and digital assets: A newer, more volatile space. I tell clients to only invest money they can afford to lose, and to spend as much time learning about it as they do putting money in.

Exploring Other Alternatives – At a Glance

Property (Direct Ownership) – Buying residential or commercial property to generate rental income and/or long-term capital growth.

REITs (Real Estate Investment Trusts) – Pooled funds that invest in property, offering easier access, dividends, and liquidity compared to owning property directly.

Property Crowdfunding – Online platforms allowing small-scale investments into real estate projects without owning the whole property.

Commodities – Exposure to raw materials like gold, oil, or agricultural goods. Can hedge against inflation but often volatile.

Collectibles – Tangible items like art, antiques, wine, or classic cars that may appreciate but require specialist knowledge and patience.

Private Equity – Investing in private companies not listed on the stock market, usually via specialist funds. Higher risk but potentially higher reward.

Venture Capital / Angel Investing – Backing early-stage businesses. Exciting growth potential, but high risk of losing capital.

Hedge Funds – Specialist funds using complex strategies (like short-selling or leverage). Usually only available to high-net-worth investors.

Cryptocurrency & Digital Assets – Highly speculative investments in digital currencies (e.g., Bitcoin) or blockchain projects. High volatility, only suitable for money you can afford to lose.

Infrastructure Funds – Investments in roads, energy, utilities, and other large-scale projects that can provide steady long-term returns.

Peer-to-Peer Lending – Providing loans via online platforms, earning interest in return. Attractive yields but carries default risk.

PROCEED WITH CAUTION

Alternative investments can diversify a portfolio and sometimes deliver strong returns, but they often carry higher risks, lower liquidity, and more complexity than traditional investments. Before committing, consider how they fit with your overall financial plan and risk tolerance and seek expert advice if you're unsure.

How Alternatives Fit Into Your Bigger Plan

Alternative investments usually work best as the icing on your financial cake, not the cake itself. Most advisers recommend keeping them to 10–20% of your total portfolio as a maximum. They can be exciting and potentially lucrative, but they're often less liquid, meaning you can't sell them quickly without affecting the price.

Tax rules vary widely depending on the asset, and can make a huge difference to your returns, so a good tax adviser is worth their weight in gold here too.

Perhaps most importantly, build your expertise in one area before rushing into others. Mastering a single niche is far more sustainable than chasing every "hot" opportunity you hear about.

Managing Risk in Alternative Spaces

The less traditional an investment is, the more important your due diligence becomes. You'll need to know:

- What drives its value
- The main risks and how they show up
- How quickly you could sell it if needed
- How you'll measure whether it's performing as expected
- The costs of investing or disinvesting

Reliable information can be harder to find in these spaces, so seek out industry publications, knowledgeable communities, and ideally, people who've been doing it successfully for years. Of course, this is one of the reasons we started Eva Wealth and there is a whole host of information that you can find at your fingertips at **evawealth.co.uk** and **mywealthvault.co.uk**.

And if you're serious, pair your general financial plan with specialist advice for that particular type of investment. That combination of breadth and depth is where most long-term success stories come from.

Final thought: Property and alternative investments can bring valuable diversity to your wealth plan, but only if they're well-researched, well-timed, and well-integrated with everything else you're doing. The thrill of the unusual should never outweigh the need for balance. If you keep that in mind, these assets can add both stability and spark to your financial future.

Chapter 11 Workbook Exercises: Property And Alternative Investments

1. **Quick Knowledge Check:** Beyond traditional shares and bonds, I'm most interested in:
   - ☐ Buy-to-let property
   - ☐ REITs
   - ☐ Commodities
   - ☐ Collectibles
   - ☐ None appeal to me

2. **One Key Reflection:** My attitude toward alternative investments is:
   - ☐ Excited but need to learn more
   - ☐ Cautious but curious
   - ☐ Too risky for me
   - ☐ Essential for diversification

3. **Priority Action This Week:**
   - ☐ Research the tax implications of buy-to-let property
   - ☐ Calculate what deposit I'd need for investment property
   - ☐ Investigate REITs as an alternative to direct property ownership

Chapter 12:
Pension Planning with Purpose

Retirement planning is something that I love to undertake with my clients. The concept 'retirement' is a relatively new one in our history and even within my lifetime so far, I have witnessed its meaning change. 20 to 30 years ago, the concept of retirement was that you worked (often for just 1 or maybe 2 different employers) until an age the company told you was a normal age to stop and then you stopped work.

But the concept of retirement has changed – and I believe is continuing to change. For many women now, it is less about a sudden and complete stop, and more about a moving into the next phase. Often this is moving from a fast-paced, high powered job into a flexible, reduced hours role. One that you dictate the terms for. It is less about the earning potential and more about the enjoyment. It's also a time when I've witnessed beautiful mentorship taking place as capacity increases and focus changes.

So as you read this chapter, instead of using the word retirement, let's call these our wisdom years! These years for many are not always about escaping work, but creating freedom to pursue your purpose in later life. This chapter reframes pension planning as designing your future freedom.

PRESENT BIAS & FUTURE YOU

Our brains are wired to prioritise immediate rewards over future ones ("present bias"). That's why contributing to a pension feels less urgent than a weekend trip. A simple trick: picture your future self. Studies show that visualising yourself at age 70 increases your likelihood of saving more, because your brain treats "future you" as part of your identity.

Daily Newspaper

ISSUE: 131 | SUNDAY 30 NOVEMBER 6 2025 | FINANCIAL NEWS

A BRIEF HISTORY OF RETIREMENT

For most of human history, "retirement" wasn't even a word. Life was work, and work was life. People laboured in fields, households, or trades until they physically couldn't, relying on family or community to support them in later years.

It wasn't until the late 1800s that the modern idea of retirement began to take shape. In 1889, Germany's Chancellor Otto von Bismarck introduced the first state pension scheme, offering income to those over 70. Other countries gradually followed, seeing retirement as both a social good and a way to refresh the workforce with younger employees.

By the early 20th century, retirement had become part of social policy. In the UK, the first state pension was introduced in 1908 for people over 70, later reduced to 65. In the US, Social Security was established in 1935, embedding the expectation that one could eventually stop working and live on a pension.

The post-war decades transformed retirement into something more cultural than purely practical. Longer life expectancies, rising prosperity, and employer-sponsored pension schemes reframed it as a deserved period of rest, travel, and leisure after years of labour.

Today, that traditional model is shifting again. With fewer guaranteed pensions, longer lifespans, and more varied career paths, many people no longer see retirement as a single end-point. Instead, it's becoming a new life stage, what I like to call the "wisdom years"; a time to choose how you spend your energy, whether that means part-time work, volunteering, launching a business, or simply enjoying freedom on your own terms.

Reimagining Later Life

Moving beyond retirement stereotypes opens new possibilities for re-envisioning your wisdom years. Rather than viewing retirement as withdrawal from productive life, many women are creating third acts that combine purpose, pleasure, and continued contribution. More businesses are being launched aligned with lifelong passions, others deepen community involvement, while many create flexible arrangements blending part-time work with increased leisure.

Creating a purpose-driven later life begins with reflection on what brings you meaning:

- What activities engage you so deeply that time seems to disappear?
- What contributions do you hope to make?
- What relationships do you wish to nurture?
- What bucket list items will you have still on your list to experience?

Asking these questions is a core part of my work with clients because reflecting on these creates the foundation for planning your wisdom years that serve your deeper aspirations.

Understanding your "freedom number", the financial resources needed for your vision, requires translating your purpose-driven plan into financial terms. This goes beyond standard retirement calculators to consider the specific resources your unique vision requires. If your desire is to travel the world twice over and never work again, you are going to need very different financial resources from someone who is looking to enjoy countryside walks from home whilst running yoga retreats from a studio in her garden in the Somerset countryside.

Regardless of your vision, we all share a common need. That is the requirement on us to fund these years. The State Pension is insufficient on its own to meet most people's typical living costs. Furthermore, due to the different challenges women typically face during their working lives, it may be that you haven't accrued sufficient credits during your working life to secure the maximum state pension. So the responsibility sits on each of our shoulders to make sure we are providing the financial means to fund our desired future.

Building flexibility for life's evolutions acknowledges that your vision at 40 may differ from your reality at 65. Effective wisdom years planning creates options rather than locking you into a single path. This might mean developing multiple income streams, maintaining marketable skills, and preserving some financial capacity for life's unexpected turns.

THE FEMALE MATRIARCH: A LESSON FROM THE WILD

Elephant herds are matriarchal, usually led by the oldest and most experienced female. Her role is not one of dominance in the aggressive sense, but rather of **guidance, decision-making, and protection**.

The matriarch:

- **Decides when and where to travel**, especially in times of scarcity.
- **Holds a memory map** of watering holes, feeding grounds, and safe routes, sometimes remembered from decades earlier.
- **Provides social stability**, mediating disputes, comforting distressed members, and teaching younger elephants.
- **Protects against threats** by recognising signs of danger (such as predators or poachers) and guiding the herd's response.

Wisdom Years in Action

One striking example of wisdom years is during drought. A younger leader may not remember a faraway water source that saved the herd decades ago. A matriarch, however, might guide them to it, ensuring survival. Studies show herds led by older matriarchs have higher survival rates, especially in crises.

Her wisdom isn't just geographical, it extends to **social knowledge.** Matriarchs can distinguish friend from foe, recall the calls of hundreds of elephants, and judge the seriousness of threats. This stored experience helps the herd avoid unnecessary fights and conserve energy.

What We Can Learn

The elephant matriarch is often used as a metaphor for leadership in human communities:

- Leadership based on **memory, wisdom, and compassion** rather than brute force.
- The idea that **later life can be a time of power and respect**, where accumulated experiences serve not just the individual but the wider group.
- The matriarch embodies a **fusion of strength and nurturing**, a balance many cultures admire.

Understanding Pension Fundamentals

Workplace pensions are often the backbone of retirement planning, yet I've found that many people don't fully understand how they work. This lack of knowledge can really limit both our planning and our freedom. That's why it's so important to get familiar with your own scheme, whether it's defined benefit, defined contribution, or a hybrid. Each type comes with its own opportunities and constraints. Most of us are automatically enrolled into a default option, but there are usually choices you can make that have a big impact: increasing contributions, selecting different investment funds, or understanding how life events such as parental leave affect your pension. Every one of these factors influences the size of your final pot and the income it can provide. The more we understand, the better we can shape our pension to support the future we want.

Personal pension options provide flexibility beyond workplace provisions. These self-directed plans offer control over contribution levels, investment selections, and eventually, withdrawal strategies. For those of us with variable income, career breaks, or entrepreneurial aspirations, personal pensions often play an especially important role in creating financial security. As a business owner, there can be significant benefits to boosting your pension contributions and receiving attractive tax relief. You can even use your pension to buy your business property. So, building up your pension with contributions in the early years increases the options available to you in the future when these opportunities arise.

Currently, state pension entitlements form an important base layer of retirement income. It's important not to overlook this provision. Understanding your projected entitlement, options for enhancing it through additional contributions if you have missed any accrual years, and how it integrates with your other pension provisions creates a more complete picture of your future resources. The first place to start is to request a state pension forecast from the gov.uk website as this will show you how many years you have accrued, whether you have a shortfall and how you can go about topping your state pension up.

Another important factor to consider is the impact on your state pension accrual of taking a break from work. Whilst taking a break for travel or other lifestyle choices will need to be factored into making additional personal provision for these years, taking time out of work to raise children is treated slightly differently. Currently, if you are registered to receive child benefit, you will receive state pension accrual, even if you are not working and paying national insurance contributions. This in itself can raise questions for higher income families where perhaps you have chosen not to receive child benefit in order to avoid the tax charge. Seeking additional advice around this area may be beneficial for you as the pros and cons can start to become interwoven with other personal factors.

The final point of note around pensions at a general level is that pension consolidation and management becomes increasingly important as careers become more varied. With workplace pensions, it is more common now to accumulate multiple pension pots through different employers or phases of self-employment. While consolidation sometimes offers advantages in simplicity and potentially reduced fees, each pension requires careful evaluation of benefits that might be lost through transfer.

TECHNICAL SUMMARY

Pensions are simply investment vehicles which are designed for long term investment in order to provide you with an income in retirement.

They receive attractive tax benefits on both monies paid in as well as monies paid out.

You typically get to choose how you want your pension to be invested and so can control how much growth potential and fluctuation in value your pension can experience.

It is important to make sure that you notify your pension provider of your beneficiaries so that they are able to direct your benefits to who you choose if you were to die.

Constructing Your Pension Portfolio

When you first join a pension, you'll usually be placed into a "default" fund. Think of it like being seated at the table the restaurant assumes you'll like best; convenient, but not necessarily the one with the view you'd have chosen. By taking time to understand the different investment options and why some might suit you better than others, you give your pension a much better chance of working hard for your future.

Your approach to investing will naturally evolve over time. In your earlier decades, growth-oriented investments can be powerful because you've got the longest runway; plenty of time for your money to recover from market bumps and benefit from compounding growth. Later in life, the emphasis usually shifts towards preservation and income, much like moving from climbing a mountain at pace to carefully navigating the descent. This isn't about rigid age rules, but about matching your investment strategy to your own time horizon and life stage.

Finding the right balance between growth and security is personal. For example, an individual with other substantial assets or a defined benefit pension might comfortably keep her pension invested for growth well into later years. Someone relying solely on a defined contribution pension may need a more cautious balance. It's less about formulas, and more about designing a mix that reflects your circumstances.

The good news is that pensions today also offer far more scope to invest in line with your values. You can choose ESG-integrated funds or even specialist options focused on climate solutions or gender equity, so your money not only supports your retirement, but also the kind of world you'd like to retire into.

And if your life crosses borders, whether through work, relocation, or family, pensions can become more complex. Different countries have different rules on entitlements, taxation, and withdrawals. Here, early planning with the right advice is worth its weight in gold. It can save you from costly mistakes later and make sure your future freedom isn't tied up in red tape.

The Middle Years Strategy

Career breaks often leave dents in pension savings, and for women, this is a common story. Think of it like missing a few bricks in a wall – the structure is still there, but it's weaker unless you go back and reinforce it. Proactive planning in the middle years is your chance to fill those gaps. That might mean increasing your own contributions, setting up spousal contributions where possible, or finding creative ways to add extra building blocks into your retirement pot.

The middle years can feel like a financial juggling act. Expenses are often at their highest; children's education, a mortgage, maybe even helping ageing parents, all competing with the need to save for your future. It's tempting to focus on one goal at a time, but pensions benefit most from steady, parallel progress. Imagine trying to spin multiple plates: if you let one stop entirely, it's harder to get it going again. Small, consistent contributions across different goals often create stronger outcomes than an "all or nothing" approach.

These years are also, for many women, the most powerful for pension building. Your 40s and 50s can represent peak earning potential. Directing bonuses, pay rises, or even windfalls like an inheritance into your pension during this stage is like adding high-octane fuel to your retirement engine, the effect compounds significantly down the road.

Approaching the Transition

Retirement no longer needs to be an overnight stop. For many, it looks more like crossing a series of stepping-stones than walking off a cliff. Phased retirement – working reduced hours, consulting, job-sharing, or taking on seasonal projects – provides income while keeping you connected and purposeful. It may also mean picking up new skills or exploring fresh directions that offer flexibility as well as fulfilment.

When it comes to drawing income, there's no one-size-fits-all formula. Old rules of thumb (like "take 4% a year") often miss the nuances of individual lives. Your approach should reflect what matters most: do you want stability above all, maximum flexibility, or to prioritise leaving a legacy? Think of it like designing a personal income recipe, blending different ingredients – pensions, investments, rental income, part-time work – in the proportions that suit your taste.

Tax planning plays a surprisingly big role here. Deciding which pots of money to draw from, and when, can significantly affect how long your resources last. Coordinating withdrawals across pensions, ISAs, and other accounts is like playing a careful game of chess – every move affects the next.

And then there's longevity risk, the very real possibility of outliving your savings. With women often living longer, this risk looms larger. Strategies to protect against it might include keeping part of your portfolio invested for growth, exploring longevity insurance products, or building several different income streams so you're not reliant on just one source.

Legacy and Inheritance Considerations

Pensions aren't just about your lifetime, they can also shape your legacy. Rules vary depending on the scheme, but planning ahead allows you to ensure your pension reflects your values as well as your relationships. Updating beneficiary forms, keeping expressions of wish current, and considering more complex structures if needed are all part of that picture.

Balancing legacy desires with personal needs is a delicate act. Many women want to provide for children or grandchildren, or leave a mark through charitable giving. But your own financial wellbeing must come first; you can't pour from an empty cup. A helpful exercise I often use with clients is defining what "enough" looks like for them. Once you're confident in your own security, you can plan your giving from a position of strength.

Family conversations around inheritance can feel awkward, but they're powerful. They move money from being a secret subject into a shared expression of values and intentions. I've seen families avoid conflict and build deeper trust simply by having these talks early.

Charitable giving through pensions can also be an elegant, tax-efficient way to extend your impact. From naming a charity as a beneficiary to making tax-free donations during your lifetime, pensions can often deliver more value to causes you care about than other types of assets. In this way, your pension doesn't just fund your future, it can help shape the world you leave behind.

NOTE ON BENEFICIARIES: Your pension doesn't automatically follow your will. Always complete (and update) your pension nomination forms to ensure your money goes where you want it to.

Workplace Pension Optimisation During Part-Time Work

Understanding pension basics is crucial, but women often face a unique challenge that traditional pension advice doesn't adequately address: the impact of part-time work on pension building. As we discussed in Chapter 2, women are significantly more likely to work part-time during their careers, often for caring responsibilities. This seemingly practical career adjustment can create a devastating long-term impact on your pension wealth.

The key insight is this: your pension contributions don't have to mirror your working hours. With strategic planning, you can maintain your pension trajectory even during part-time periods. This isn't just about avoiding pension poverty, it's about ensuring your reduced working hours don't compromise your financial independence.

The Part-Time Pension Gap

We have already seen that there is a gender wealth gap. But for women who work part-time too, there is a further compounding effect to consider:

- Part-time workers contribute 40% less to their pensions on average
- Women working part-time for 10 years can lose £100,000+ in pension wealth
- Many employers base contributions on actual salary rather than full-time equivalent

Optimisation Strategies

Salary Sacrifice Maximisation

Salary sacrifice means that you agree to reduce your salary in exchange for an increase employer pension contribution. Lots of employers offer this. You effectively "swap" part of your pay for a pension contribution.

The benefit to you is that pension contributions via salary sacrifice are taken before tax and National Insurance (NI) are calculated and so you pay less tax and NI overall. This means more of your money ends up in your pension.

If you go part-time, your pension contributions usually drop because they're based on your lower salary.

Here's an example:

Situation	Full-Time	Part-time
Salary	£40,000	£24,000
Typical 8% pension	£3,200	£1,920

However, you can choose to keep contributing at your old level (£3,200), by adjusting your salary sacrifice arrangement.

That means you:

- Maintain your pension growth trajectory (so future you doesn't "miss out" on valuable compounding)
- Pay less tax and NI now, because those contributions reduce your taxable salary.

This is ideal if you can afford to maintain contributions while working reduced hours. You earn less but keep saving at the same rate and do it in the most tax-efficient way.

The "Top-Up" Method

If salary sacrifice isn't possible or you're not employed (e.g., self-employed, or your employer scheme is inflexible), you can personally top up your pension to make up for reduced contributions. This means you can continue building your pension momentum during periods of part-time work or career breaks and still get tax relief on your contributions.

Example steps:

- Identify your shortfall: if you used to pay £3,200/year but now pay £1,920, your shortfall is £1,280.
- Set up a personal pension (SIPP or personal pension): contribute £1,280 yourself (or whatever amount you can manage).
- Claim your tax relief: if you're a basic-rate taxpayer the pension provider adds 20% automatically (so you only pay £1,024 to get £1,280 invested). If you're a higher-rate taxpayer, you can claim extra relief via your tax return.
- Review annually: adjust as your income changes or if you return to full-time work.

In short, this method keeps your pension on track through flexible, self-managed contributions. It is ideal if you can't use salary sacrifice or are self-employed.

Employer Negotiation Tactics

Questions to ask HR:

- "Can pension contributions be based on full-time equivalent salary?"
- "Are there flexible benefits that could enhance pension provision?"
- "What's the policy on maintaining benefits during part-time work?"

Case Study: Emma's Pension Protection

Situation: Reduced to 3 days/week after maternity leave

Original impact: Pension contributions down from £3,000 to £1,800

Solution implemented:

- Negotiated with employer to maintain full pension contribution
- Used childcare voucher salary sacrifice to fund difference
- Set up personal pension for extra £100/month

10-year impact: Pension back on track, saving £80,000 in lost growth

These pension protection strategies become even more critical when we consider other major life transitions. As we'll explore in Chapter 14, divorce planning must consider pensions. The habits you build now will serve you in every stage of your financial journey.

Pension Strategies by Money Personality

Your approach to pension planning should align with your money story archetype:

Status Seekers: Your pension can become your ultimate achievement. Track your projected pension pot like a scoreboard. Consider additional voluntary contributions (AVCs) as a tax-efficient way to build impressive retirement wealth. Your competitive nature helps you maximise employer matching and tax relief.

Guardians: Your pension is your ultimate security blanket. You'll likely be comfortable with higher contributions and conservative investment choices within your pension. Focus on the guaranteed aspects – employer matching, tax relief, and the security of a growing pot for your future.

Free Spirits: Connect your pension to your vision of retirement freedom. What experiences do you want your pension to fund? Consider lifestyle funds that automatically adjust risk as you age, removing the need for active management. Your pension should feel like investing in future adventures.

Avoiders: Set up your pension contributions and investment choices once, then leave them alone. Auto-escalation features that gradually increase your contributions are perfect for you. The less you need to think about it, the better – but the more it grows automatically.

Chapter 12 Workbook Exercises: Pension Planning with Purpose

1. **Quick Knowledge Check:**
   - ☐ I currently contribute _____% of my salary to my pension.
   - ☐ My workplace matching contribution is _____%
     (Don't know? Check your payslip or HR portal)

2. **One Key Reflection:** My vision for my "wisdom years" includes:

3. **Priority Action This Week:**
   - ☐ Log into my pension provider's website and review my current pot
   - ☐ Check if I'm getting full employer matching
   - ☐ Request a state pension forecast from gov.uk

Part 4: Life Transitions

"You may not control all the events that happen to you, but you can decide not to be reduced by them." -Maya Angelou

Life has a way of surprising us, doesn't it? Just when we think we've found our rhythm, something shifts. A promotion lands in our lap, we fall in love, face heartbreak, or suddenly find ourselves navigating waters we never expected. These transitions can feel disruptive, but they also hold the power to reset, refocus, and realign our financial foundations.

For women, these shifts often carry unique financial weight. Stepping back from work to care for family, merging finances with a partner, navigating divorce or bereavement, or suddenly becoming the sole decision-maker in areas we once shared, can feel overwhelming. But here's the truth I want you to carry with you: you are stronger and more capable than you know. With the right mindset and strategies, you can approach any transition not with fear, but with clarity and confidence.

This section is about preparing for, and thriving through, life's pivotal moments. We'll cover the practical steps to protect and grow your finances, but equally, we'll focus on the mindset shifts and tools that will serve you whatever life throws your way. Because transitions aren't just about surviving change, they're about using it as a stepping stone toward the life and financial future you really want.

Chapter 13:
Owning Your Worth – Career Progression and Wealth Building

The Career–Wealth Connection

Building confidence in your financial abilities, as we explored in Chapter 3, extends directly into one of the most powerful wealth-building tools available to you: your ability to negotiate your worth. Yet research shows that while women ask for raises 85% as often as men, we receive them 15% less frequently. This isn't about capability, it's about understanding the unique dynamics women face in salary negotiations and developing strategies that work with, rather than against, these realities.

Your salary isn't just your current income, it's the foundation of your lifetime wealth. A £5,000 salary increase today compounds into hundreds of thousands of pounds over your career when you factor in future raises, pension contributions, and investment opportunities. This is why mastering the art of negotiation isn't optional, it's essential for your financial rebellion.

Career decisions are rarely just financial decisions for women. They are layered with questions of childcare, alignment with values, emotional and mental load, and caring responsibilities that often fall disproportionately to us. A promotion might look great on paper, but if it means missing bedtimes five nights a week, the choice isn't straightforward. A sideways move with lower pay might feel counterintuitive, yet it could bring flexibility, purpose, or future opportunities that outweigh the short-term financial hit.

This complexity doesn't mean women are "less ambitious." It means our ambitions are more holistic. We don't just want bigger pay checks, we want balance, impact, and lives that reflect our priorities. But here's where we must be vigilant: money matters too. Every career choice has financial consequences that ripple into our pensions, savings, investments, and long-term independence.

Perhaps this balancing act helps explain in part why the gender wealth gap remains. While men's career moves are often judged by financial progression alone, women's decisions are evaluated against a far wider set of trade-offs. That doesn't make our choices wrong, but it does mean we need to approach them consciously, with eyes wide open to the financial implications alongside the emotional and practical ones.

Your career is one of the most powerful wealth-building tools you will ever have. By owning your worth, making intentional moves, and investing in yourself, you can shape not only your professional path but also the financial freedom that underpins your future.

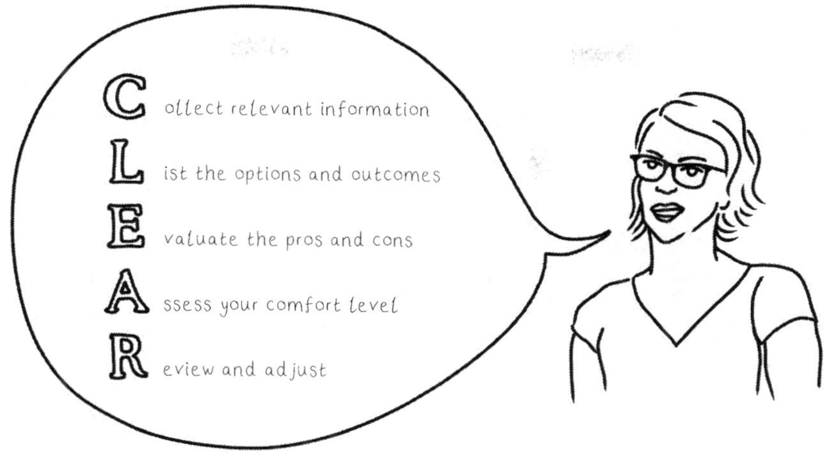

Negotiating Your Worth

Have you experienced that feeling – sat across from your manager, heart racing as you prepare to ask for a raise? Despite exceeding every target, leading projects outside your remit, and mentoring younger staff, it's a conversation that you have put off for months. Sound familiar?

Many women hesitate to negotiate, not because we lack skill, but because we've been taught to fear being seen as "pushy" or "difficult." Research shows women negotiate less often than men and, when we do, we tend to ask for less. Over time, that hesitation translates into significant lost income, lower pension contributions, and reduced financial security.

Preparing for a salary negotiation:

Remember the confidence-building CLEAR decision-making framework we developed in Chapter 3? This becomes essential when preparing for salary negotiations. The process of Collecting information, Listing options, Evaluating pros and cons, Assessing comfort levels, and Reviewing decisions will serve you well as you prepare to advocate for your worth.

Build your evidence. Document achievements, quantify impact, and research market benchmarks.

Frame the conversation around value. Instead of "I need a raise because childcare is expensive," try: "Based on my performance and the £15,000 in additional revenue I've generated this year, I believe my pay should reflect that contribution."

Reframe rejection. A no today isn't failure; it's a marker that you're advocating for yourself and laying groundwork for the next review.

Negotiating isn't just about the number on your payslip. It's about reinforcing to yourself (and others) that your work has value and deserves recognition.

EVIDENCE BOX: Why Negotiation Matters

Fewer Women Negotiate: Only 7% of women negotiate their first salary compared to 57% of men (Babcock & Laschever, Women Don't Ask). Over time, this compounds into significant income loss.

Women Ask for Less: Studies show women tend to request smaller increases and settle earlier in negotiations, limiting long-term earning growth (Gerhart & Rynes, Journal of Applied Psychology).

The Backlash Effect: Research from Harvard (Bowles, Babcock & Lai) finds women who negotiate assertively are more likely to be perceived as "pushy" or "difficult," creating a social cost men are less likely to face.

Lifetime Impact: The UK gender pay gap, currently around 14%, is partly driven by this negotiation gap, reducing women's pensions and long-term financial security (CIPD & Equalities Office research.

The Research Reality

Recent studies reveal stark differences in how salary negotiations are perceived when conducted by women versus men:

The Backlash Effect: Research by Harvard Business School shows women face social backlash when negotiating assertively, being perceived as "pushy" or "difficult" (Bowles & Babcock, 2013)

The Ask Gap: Women ask for raises 85% as often as men, but receive them 15% less frequently (Harvard Business Review, 2018)

Starting Point Impact: The initial salary offer impacts lifetime earnings by an average of £500,000+ for women due to compounding effects

Women-Specific Negotiation Strategies

The Collaborative Approach

Strategy: Frame negotiations as collaborative problem-solving rather than adversarial demands.

Script Example: "I've been researching market rates for my role and contributions. Could we explore how my compensation might better reflect the value I'm bringing to the team?"

The Research-Heavy Method

Strategy: Come armed with extensive data to counteract the "she's being emotional" bias.

Preparation Toolkit:

- Industry salary surveys (Glassdoor, PayScale, professional associations)
- Internal equity analysis (if accessible)
- Achievement quantification (revenue generated, costs saved, efficiency improvements)
- Market comparison data

The Advocate Approach

Strategy: Position the request as advocacy for team/company success rather than personal gain.

Example: "Ensuring fair compensation helps our team attract and retain top talent. I'd like to discuss how we can position my role competitively."

Case Study: Sarah's Strategic Success

Background: Marketing manager, 3 years experience, 20% below market rate

Challenge: Previous negotiation attempts dismissed as "not being realistic"

Strategy:

- Documented 6 months of achievements with revenue impact (£150k new business)
- Researched 5 comparable roles in similar companies
- Identified mentor willing to provide reference letter
- Scheduled meeting during positive project outcome period

Outcome: 18% salary increase + performance bonus structure

Key Factor: Timing + data + collaborative framing

Strategic Career Moves

Armed with negotiation skills and confidence in your worth, you're well-positioned to build wealth throughout your career. But what happens when your career path includes those times when your path might not follow the traditional linear progression. What about the breaks and adjustments that often come with motherhood? As we calculated in Chapter 2, career breaks can have significant long-term financial impacts, but they don't have to derail your wealth-building journey if you approach them strategically.

The key is shifting from seeing career breaks as interruptions to viewing them as strategic pauses that you can navigate without sacrificing your long-term financial goals. This requires planning, creativity, and sometimes, challenging conventional thinking about what career progression looks like.

Career growth is rarely a straight ladder climb. For us as women, it can feel more like a winding path: sideways moves, pauses, pivots, and reinventions. Each step has a financial implication (alongside all the other considerations we are often juggling at the same time), and being strategic makes the difference between a short-term setback and a long-term leap.

The sideways move. It may be that you accept a role with a £3,000 pay cut, but because it comes with funded training, flexible hours, and a clear promotion path. Eighteen months later, it may be that you are promoted with a £12,000 increase, more than offsetting the initial dip, while giving you a stronger foundation for future growth.

Career breaks. Many women step back from the workforce for caregiving, health, or personal reasons. While breaks can impact earnings and pensions, they don't have to derail your financial future. Keeping professional connections alive through freelance projects, short courses, or volunteering keeps your skills current and your confidence intact.

Reinvention later in life. For many women, the biggest career acceleration comes once family responsibilities ease. These years can be powerful for boosting savings, topping up pensions, and investing for independence. A career "second act" can feel like a reset button, both personally and financially.

Building Strategic Additional Income Streams

Creating multiple income streams isn't about working endless hours, it's about building financial resilience and leveraging your skills beyond traditional employment. The key is approaching additional income strategically, ensuring each stream aligns with your goals and available bandwidth.

Skills Audit and Monetisation Strategy

Begin with an honest assessment of your marketable skills. What do colleagues ask for your help with? What problems do you solve naturally? What knowledge do you possess that others value? Your most profitable side ventures often emerge from expertise you already possess rather than entirely new endeavours.

Consider both direct monetisation (consulting, freelancing, teaching) and indirect approaches (creating products, building assets, developing passive income streams). Direct monetisation typically generates income faster, while indirect approaches can create longer-term value.

The Service-to-Product Evolution

Many successful female entrepreneurs begin by selling their time through services, then evolve to selling their knowledge through products. A marketing consultant might start with client work, then create templates, courses, or automated services that generate income without requiring her direct time.

This evolution allows you to scale beyond the natural limits of hourly work while building intellectual property that has ongoing value. Document your processes, create templates, and identify recurring problems you solve, these often become your most valuable products.

Technology Tools for Efficiency

Modern technology enables one-person businesses to operate with unprecedented efficiency. Automation tools can handle scheduling, payments, customer communication, and basic marketing tasks, freeing you to focus on high-value activities.

Start simple with basic tools for the functions that consume most of your administrative time, then gradually expand your technology stack as your business grows. The goal is creating systems that work without your constant attention.

Managing the Employment Relationship

Before launching any side venture, understand your employment contract and company policies. Many employers have restrictions on external business activities, particularly in related fields. Being transparent about your plans and ensuring compliance protects both your current employment and your entrepreneurial ventures.

Consider intellectual property implications carefully. Work created on company time or using company resources typically belongs to your employer, even if it's unrelated to your job. Keep your side ventures clearly separate from your employment responsibilities.

Financial Management for Multiple Income Streams

Variable income requires different financial management approaches than steady employment. Build larger emergency funds to account for income volatility, and develop cash flow forecasting skills to anticipate lean periods.

Separate business and personal finances from the beginning, even for simple side hustles. This simplifies tax preparation, provides clearer financial pictures, and establishes good habits if your ventures grow.

Track time investment alongside financial returns. A side hustle generating £500 monthly might seem attractive until you calculate you're earning £5 per hour. Understanding your true hourly rate helps you make informed decisions about continuing, scaling, or pivoting.

Tax Optimisation for Entrepreneurs

Multiple income streams create tax planning opportunities unavailable to traditional employees. Business expenses can often be deducted against income, and pension contributions from business profits can provide significant tax advantages.

However, complexity increases with multiple income sources. Consider professional tax advice once your additional income reaches meaningful levels, as the savings often exceed the advisory costs.

Scaling and Exit Strategies

Plan for success from the beginning. What would happen if your side hustle became more profitable than your primary employment? How would you scale operations? What systems would need to be in place?

Many women underestimate their potential and fail to plan for growth, creating bottlenecks that limit their success. Thinking through scaling challenges early allows you to build foundations that support growth rather than constraining it.

Investing in Yourself

The most important investment you will ever make is in yourself. Qualifications, professional development, networks, and personal brand all directly influence your earning power.

Ask yourself: *Will this course, event, or opportunity expand my options or earning potential?* If yes, it's likely a worthwhile investment.

Strategic education. Don't just chase certificates, evaluate the return on investment.

Networking. Build relationships, not just contacts. Many opportunities flow through personal recommendations.

Personal brand. In today's digital world, your online presence matters. Position yourself as a thought leader in your field and watch doors open more easily.

Every pound invested in your development can multiply across the years in higher earnings, greater opportunities, and stronger financial independence.

But it can be a difficult decision to make when you're at the start point looking forward and wondering about the commitment of finance and time.

Planning for the Unexpected

Careers rarely run smoothly forever. Economic downturns, restructures, industry changes, or health challenges can all shift the ground beneath you. Preparation creates resilience.

Emergency fund. Aim for 6–12 months of expenses if you're in a volatile sector or self-employed.

Transferable skills. Focus on strengths resistant to automation: leadership, problem-solving, emotional intelligence.

Continuous learning. Stay relevant by upskilling regularly. The world of work changes fast, staying ahead keeps you employable and confident.

Owning your worth means honouring both sides of the equation: the emotional, practical, and personal factors that shape your career decisions and the financial consequences that follow. By making conscious, strategic choices, you're not only shaping your professional story, you're building the wealth and independence that give you true freedom.

Your career is one of your most powerful wealth-building tools, and protecting its trajectory, even during breaks and transitions, is essential for your financial independence. Whether through strategic negotiations, planned career breaks, or pension protection during part-time work, you have the tools to ensure your career serves your wealth-building goals.

In our next chapter, we'll explore another crucial aspect of financial planning that affects many women: navigating the financial complexities of marriage and divorce.

Chapter 13 Workbook Exercises: Career Progression And Wealth Building

1. **Quick Knowledge Check:** I last negotiated my salary:
   - ☐ This year
   - ☐ 1–2 years ago
   - ☐ 3+ years ago
   - ☐ Never

2. **One Key Reflection:** My biggest career-related financial challenge is:
   - ☐ Asking for what I'm worth
   - ☐ Planning for career breaks
   - ☐ Building multiple income streams
   - ☐ Investing in my skills

3. **Priority Action This Week:**
   - ☐ Research market rates for my role and experience
   - ☐ Update my CV and LinkedIn profile
   - ☐ Identify one way to increase my income this year

Chapter 14:
Marriage, Divorce and Your Money

The Financial Side of Love

Money and relationships are inextricably linked, and nowhere is this more evident than in marriage and divorce. While we hope for lifelong partnerships, the reality is that divorce affects 42% of marriages in the UK, and women often face unique financial challenges during this transition. Understanding your financial rights and options isn't pessimistic, it's empowering preparation that ensures you can navigate any life change with confidence.

This chapter will guide you through both the collaborative financial planning that strengthens marriages and the strategic thinking needed if relationships end. Remember, knowledge is power, and financial knowledge is financial power.

DECISION FATIGUE IN TRANSITION

During major life changes, your brain is bombarded with decisions, which can deplete mental energy. This decision fatigue makes you more likely to default to inaction, or accept choices that aren't ideal. Breaking decisions into smaller, manageable steps helps reduce overwhelm and improves clarity.

Merging Lives and Finances

Moving in together or getting married is exciting, but it also raises financial complexity. Suddenly, you're not just managing your own money. You're merging different money stories, spending habits, and financial priorities.

The Money Conversation

Before you merge accounts or sign joint agreements, create space for an open and honest conversation:

- What debts do you each carry?
- What savings, pensions, or investments exist?
- What are your financial goals for the next 5, 10, and 20 years?

These aren't always easy questions. For many women, money can carry shame or fear, especially if you've been taught not to talk about it. Approach the conversation with curiosity, not criticism.

As we've already seen at the very beginning of this book, our own money stories play a huge role in our relationship with money. Don't underestimate the impact of now trying to combine two sets of money stories! I strongly advocate exploring your money personalities together as a couple and discussing the behavioural similarities and differences that this can highlight.

TIP: Try framing it as a "finance date night" – a glass of wine, a calm environment, and a commitment to listen without judgement.

Designing Your Financial Structure

There's no single "right" way to manage money as a couple. What matters is finding an approach that supports both independence and shared goals.

Fully Joint: All income and expenses are shared.

Fully Separate: Each manages their own money, with bills divided.

Hybrid: A joint account for shared expenses, plus individual accounts for personal spending.

The Three-Account System

This hybrid structure allows you to:

- Maintain your own account for personal independence.
- Share a joint account for household bills.
- Contribute proportionally (not always equally) if incomes differ.

This is especially important for women who may take career breaks – proportional contributions acknowledge both financial and non-financial contributions.

Money Conversations by Personality: Scripts That Work

How you approach money conversations with your partner depends heavily on your money story archetype. Here are specific scripts and strategies:

Status Seeker Conversation Approaches

Your Challenge: You might worry about appearing controlling or materialistic when discussing financial goals.

Effective Opening Scripts:

- **For goal-setting:** "I've been thinking about our financial future, and I'd love to share some goals I'm excited about. I know we both want to be successful, so let's talk about what financial success looks like for us as a couple."
- **For spending concerns:** "I've noticed I sometimes spend money to feel successful, and I want to be more intentional about that. Can we talk about what purchases actually align with our long-term goals?"
- **For investment discussions:** "I'm excited about building real wealth together. What would it feel like to have enough investments that we never had to worry about money again?"

Key Strategies:

- Frame financial goals as achievements to unlock together
- Share your motivation for building wealth beyond appearances
- Ask about their financial goals and dreams
- Focus on team success rather than individual control

Guardian Conversation Approaches

Your Challenge: You might come across as overly cautious or controlling about spending.

Effective Opening Scripts:

- **For budget discussions:** "I feel most comfortable when we have a clear picture of our finances. Could we review our budget together so we both feel secure about our spending?"
- **For spending concerns:** "I sometimes worry about money more than I need to. Can you help me understand your perspective on this purchase so we can find a balance?"
- **For savings goals:** "I love knowing we're prepared for whatever comes our way. What would make you feel most financially secure?"

Key Strategies:

- Acknowledge your cautious nature as care, not control
- Ask for their input on what feels like "enough" security
- Share the anxiety behind your caution
- Create spending categories you both feel good about

Free Spirit Conversation Approaches

Your Challenge: You might seem irresponsible or dismissive of financial planning.

Effective Opening Scripts:

- **For budget discussions:** "I know I sometimes spend impulsively, and I want us to find a way to plan that still feels flexible and fun. What would a budget look like that we'd both actually enjoy following?"
- **For savings goals:** "I love experiences and being generous, and I also want us to have financial freedom. How can we save for our future while still enjoying life now?"
- **For spending explanations:** "I realise my spending might seem random, but it usually connects to something I value. Let me explain my thinking, and I'd love to hear your perspective too."

Key Strategies:

- Connect financial planning to experiences and values you both care about
- Suggest automated systems that preserve spontaneity
- Acknowledge the valid concerns behind their caution
- Focus on how good planning enables more generosity and experiences

Avoider Conversation Approaches

Your Challenge: You might seem disengaged or unwilling to take responsibility.

Effective Opening Scripts:

- **For starting money talks:** "I know I usually avoid money conversations, but I care about our future together. Could we start with something small and build up to bigger financial discussions?"
- **For sharing financial anxiety:** "Money conversations make me anxious, but avoiding them makes things worse. Can we find a way to talk about this that feels supportive rather than overwhelming?"
- **For decision-making:** "I tend to avoid financial decisions because they feel overwhelming. Could you help me break this down into smaller steps so I can participate more?"

Key Strategies:

- Be honest about your avoidance patterns
- Ask for patience and support in building financial engagement
- Suggest starting with small, manageable topics
- Request regular check-ins to build the habit gradually

Universal Conversation Principles

Before any money conversation:

- Choose a calm, private moment
- Acknowledge that money conversations can be emotional
- Agree to listen without judgment
- Set a specific time limit to prevent overwhelm

During the conversation:

- Use "I" statements about your feelings and concerns
- Ask open-ended questions about their perspective
- Summarise what you heard before responding
- Take breaks if emotions get high

After the conversation:

- Summarise any decisions or next steps
- Schedule follow-up conversations for complex topics
- Appreciate their willingness to engage
- Start with small actions rather than dramatic changes

SAMPLE COMPLETE CONVERSATION: DIFFERENT ARCHETYPE COUPLE

Scenario: Guardian (Sarah) wants to discuss Free Spirit partner (Mike) spending on dining out.

Sarah (Guardian): "Mike, I've been looking at our budget, and I'm feeling a bit anxious about our dining out spending. I know you love trying new restaurants, and I don't want to take that joy away. Could we talk about finding a balance that helps me feel secure while still letting you enjoy experiences?"

Mike (Free Spirit): "I appreciate you saying it that way. I do love trying new places – it's how I connect with friends and explore the city. What specifically is worrying you?"

Sarah: "We spent £400 on dining out last month, and our budget was £200. I'm worried we're not saving enough for emergencies. What would it feel like to have a set amount we could spend guilt-free on restaurants?"

Mike: "I hadn't realised it was that much. I love the idea of guilt-free spending – that actually sounds more enjoyable than constantly wondering if I should be spending this money. What amount would help you feel secure?"

Sarah: "What if we planned for £250 for dining out, and I set up an automatic transfer to savings so I know we're still building our emergency fund?"

Mike: "That works for me. And maybe I could help by suggesting some less expensive places sometimes, or cooking at home more often when it's just us."

This conversation works because:

- Sarah acknowledged Mike's values (experiences, connection)
- Mike didn't get defensive about his spending
- They found a solution that addressed both needs
- They ended with specific, actionable steps

Protecting Your Financial Independence

Even in the happiest relationship, maintaining your own financial identity matters. For women, this is particularly crucial because too often, independence has been quietly surrendered in the name of love.

Credit History: Keep at least one account in your name.

Personal Savings: Build a small, ring-fenced fund for your own needs and peace of mind.

Stay Informed: Don't hand over financial management entirely. You deserve clarity on your full financial picture; investments, pensions, insurance, and debts.

This isn't about preparing for divorce. It's also not about both of you being fully involved in all the finances – it makes sense in a partnership to delegate the roles according to interests, skills and time. But, it is about ensuring resilience if illness, job loss, or bereavement changes your circumstances and making sure you are in the know.

Recognising and Addressing Financial Abuse

TRIGGER WARNING & SAFETY NOTICE

CONTENT WARNING & SAFETY NOTICE
This section addresses financial abuse, which may be triggering for some readers. If you are currently experiencing abuse, please prioritise your safety above all else.

IMMEDIATE SAFETY: If you are in immediate danger, call 999 (emergency services) or 101 (non-emergency police).

DIGITAL SAFETY: If you're concerned about your online activity being monitored:

- Use a safe computer/device (library, friend's house, work)
- Clear your browsing history after reading this
- Consider accessing this content from a safe location

CONFIDENTIAL SUPPORT:

- **National Domestic** Abuse Helpline: 0808 2000 247 (free, 24 hours)
- **Men's Advice Line:** 0808 8010 327
- **Galop (LGBTQ+ domestic abuse):** 0800 999 5428

Remember: You are not alone, and this is not your fault.

Financial abuse is a form of domestic abuse that affects millions of women, cutting across all socioeconomic levels. It involves controlling a person's access to financial resources as a way of maintaining power and control in a relationship. Understanding and recognising financial abuse is crucial for every woman, whether for your own protection or to support others.

Understanding Financial Abuse Tactics

Financial abuse takes many forms, some obvious and others subtle. Obvious forms include preventing you from working, stealing your money, or refusing to let you access bank accounts. Subtle forms might include scrutinising every purchase, using financial information to track your movements, or accumulating debt in your name without your knowledge.

Isolation tactics often accompany financial abuse. An abusive partner might discourage career advancement, limit your access to transportation, or create situations where you become financially dependent. This dependency then becomes a tool for control.

Economic sabotage involves deliberate actions to damage your financial stability or credit. This might include hiding assets during separation, providing false information to credit agencies, or interfering with your employment through harassment or showing up at your workplace.
Financial abuse affects 1 in 5 adults in the UK, cutting across all income levels, educational backgrounds, and social groups. Abusers often target successful, intelligent women precisely because they have resources worth controlling.

If you recognise these patterns, you're not 'overreacting' or 'too sensitive.' Financial abuse is a recognised form of domestic abuse, and your experiences are valid.

Protection Strategies Within Relationships

Maintaining some financial independence within any relationship isn't distrust, it's wisdom. This might include maintaining individual savings accounts, keeping some assets in your name only, or maintaining your own credit history.

Document everything. Keep copies of important financial documents in a safe location outside your home. This includes bank statements, tax returns, insurance policies, and proof of income. If you suspect financial abuse, documentation becomes crucial for both protection and potential legal action.

Build and maintain your professional network and skills. Even in the happiest relationships, circumstances can change. Maintaining your ability to support yourself provides both security and confidence.

ESCALATION RISK: Taking financial independence steps can sometimes trigger increased controlling behaviour or violence from an abusive partner. This is not your fault, but it's important to have safety plans in place before taking action.

Building a Safety Fund

If you're experiencing or at risk of financial abuse, a secret safety fund can provide crucial options. This needs to be money your abuser cannot access or trace. Consider opening an account at a different bank, perhaps near your workplace, and using a trusted friend's address for statements.

Even small amounts add up over time. If you can only save £10 per month, do it. This fund isn't just about leaving, it's about having options and reducing the power money has over your situation.

Cash hidden in secure locations can provide immediate access in emergencies. This might include money for transportation, temporary accommodation, or basic necessities.

SAFETY FIRST: Only attempt these strategies if it's safe to do so. If your partner monitors your activities closely, any of these actions could escalate the situation. Trust your instincts about what's safe.

Safety Planning Checklist

1. Identify safe places you could go quickly
2. Have a bag packed with essentials (hidden safely)
3. Know who you could call for help
4. Have important documents copied/stored safely
5. Plan escape routes from your home/work

Recovery and Rebuilding Framework

Recovery from financial abuse involves both practical and emotional work. Practically, you may need to rebuild credit, establish independent accounts, and develop new income sources. Emotionally, you may need to rebuild your relationship with money and your confidence in financial decision-making.

Start with immediate safety and basic needs. Secure housing, income, and essential services take priority over long-term financial planning. Once basic stability is established, you can begin building toward your future goals.

Credit repair often requires patience and persistence. Dispute fraudulent accounts, establish new positive credit history, and consider professional help if the damage is extensive. Credit can be rebuilt, even from significant damage.

Your strength: Reading this section took courage. Recognising financial abuse patterns shows remarkable awareness and strength. Many women who have experienced financial abuse go on to build extraordinary financial independence and help others on similar journeys.

Recovery is possible: With the right support, trauma-informed therapy, and specialised financial guidance, you can rebuild both your financial security and your relationship with money. Your future is not defined by your past experiences.

Continue your journey: The other chapters in this book contain strategies that can support your recovery and long-term financial empowerment. Take what serves you, and always prioritise your safety and wellbeing.

Professional Support Networks:

Financial abuse recovery often requires specialised support. Look for financial advisors trained in trauma-informed approaches, legal professionals experienced with financial abuse cases, and counsellors who understand the intersection of money and abuse.

Many women feel shame about financial abuse, but this is never justified. Abusers are skilled at manipulation and often target successful, intelligent women. Seeking help demonstrates strength, not weakness.

Here are some specialists who can provide you with support:

Domestic Abuse Specialists:

- Women's Aid: 0808 2000 247 – Can help with safety planning, legal rights, and financial advocacy
- Refuge: 0808 2000 247 – Emergency accommodation and support services
- Rights of Women: 020 7251 6577 – Free legal advice on family law, domestic violence

Financial Abuse Specialists:

- Surviving Economic Abuse: Resources and advocacy specifically for financial abuse
- Citizens Advice: Free, confidential advice on debt, benefits, and legal rights
- Financial Ombudsman: If financial institutions have failed to protect you

Trauma-Informed Financial Advisors:

Look for financial advisors who specifically mention experience with domestic abuse survivors or trauma-informed practice. This ensures they understand the unique challenges you face.

QUICK REFERENCE – CONFIDENTIAL SUPPORT

Emergency: 999

National Domestic Abuse Helpline: 0808 2000 247 (24/7, free)

Live Chat: nationaldahelpline.org.uk

Men's Advice Line: 0808 8010 327

LGBTQ+ Support (Galop): 0800 999 5428

Economic Abuse Specialist: survivingeconomicabuse.org

Legal Support: Rights of Women 020 7251 6577

Remember: These calls don't appear on phone bills, and websites can be accessed privately from safe devices.

Long-term Wealth Building After Abuse:

Once immediate stability is achieved, focus on building long-term financial security. This often means starting over financially, but it also means building wealth aligned with your values and goals rather than someone else's control.

Many survivors become particularly focused on financial independence, viewing wealth building as protection against future vulnerability. This can be a powerful motivator, but balance security planning with living fully in the present.

Consider how your experience might help others. Many financial abuse survivors become advocates, volunteers, or professionals helping other women. This isn't obligation, it's opportunity to transform painful experience into meaningful contribution.

IMPORTANT DISCLAIMER: The information in this section is for educational purposes only and should not replace professional advice from domestic abuse specialists, legal professionals, or law enforcement. Every situation is unique, and what works for one person may not be safe for another. Please prioritise your safety and seek professional guidance specific to your circumstances.

If you are in immediate danger, contact emergency services immediately.

When Relationships End

No one enters a marriage expecting it to end, but divorce rates remain high. For women, separation can be particularly disruptive, not just financially, but emotionally.

First Steps if You Separate

- Secure important documents (bank statements, pensions, property deeds).
- Protect your access to funds.
- Change passwords for online accounts.
- Avoid closing joint accounts without advice, as it could be legally challenged.

Understanding Your Rights

In the UK, divorce law looks at fairness, not strict 50/50. Factors include:

- Length of marriage
- Financial and non-financial contributions (yes, raising children counts)
- Future needs of each person

This is why women should never undervalue their unpaid contribution to a marriage.

Mediation vs Litigation

Mediation can often be less costly and less combative than going to court. It gives you both more control, but it only works if both partners are willing to engage.

Pension Sharing – The Hidden Asset

Pensions are often the largest asset after property, yet frequently overlooked in divorce settlements.

Understanding Your Rights

- **Pension Sharing Orders:** Can transfer percentage of ex-spouse's pension to your name
- **Pension Attachment Orders:** Provides income when pension is drawn
- **Offsetting:** Trading pension rights for other assets

Valuation Complexity

Different pension types require different approaches:

- **Defined Benefit**: Requires actuarial valuation (typically £12–£20k value per £1k annual pension)
- **Defined Contribution:** Current pot value + projected growth
- **State Pension:** Cannot be shared but affects overall planning

Property Decisions Framework

The 5-Factor Analysis:

- Affordability: Can you maintain mortgage payments solo?
- Equity Access: How much capital is locked in property?
- Future Plans: Will you need to downsize anyway?
- Children's Stability: Impact of moving vs. financial stress
- Market Timing: Current property market conditions

Option Evaluation Matrix

Option	Pros	Cons	Best For
Keep Family Home	Stability for children, familiar area	High costs, limited liquidity	Stable income, strong attachment
Sell & Split	Clean break, liquidity, fresh start	Upheaval, market dependent	Need cash, want closure
Buy Out Ex	Full ownership, control	Requires significant cash/borrowing	High income, clear future plans

Case Study: Rachel's Strategic Divorce Planning

Assets: £280k house, £45k pension (his), £12k pension (hers), £8k savings

Challenge: Wanted to keep house but couldn't afford mortgage solo

Solution:

- Obtained pension sharing order for 60% of his pension (£27k transfer)
- Used pension transfer to reduce mortgage via equity release
- Negotiated 3-year spousal maintenance to cover mortgage transition
- Kept house, maintained children's stability, secured pension future

Rebuilding After Divorce

Divorce often leaves women rebuilding their financial lives from scratch. That can feel overwhelming, but it's also a moment of possibility. When I work with clients who are going through or have recently gone through divorce, re-establishing a financial plan is so important. But not everyone is ready straight away to start planning for the future. So I like to break it down into steps that are a bit more manageable:

Short-term: Focus initially on stability. Tackle the most pressing issues such as housing, income, and creating and understanding a budget that reflects your new reality.

Medium-term: Seek to rebuild an emergency fund appropriate for your new situation. Review your pension and make sure that your future financial situation isn't neglected at the cost of providing for now. Reset your financial goals as you settle into your new situation.

Emotional Healing: Money and emotion are deeply intertwined. If financial control or financial abuse was part of your past, therapy can be as important as financial advice.

This process can't be rushed and it is important to work at a pace that you are comfortable with. Sometimes just choosing to make a start can propel you forward and be a significant part of your onward healing process. Firms like Eva Wealth can be especially helpful for these times.

The Family Home Dilemma

One of the most common patterns I see when women go through divorce is the desire to keep the family home. This is completely understandable. For many women, especially mothers, the home represents stability for the children during an already turbulent time. It can feel like the one thing you can hold onto – a space that grounds you and gives your children continuity.

But here's the challenge: the family home is often the single biggest asset in the marriage. Prioritising it sometimes comes at the cost of other critical resources, such as pensions, investments, or accessible cash.

I've worked with women who negotiated to keep the house, only to later realise that while they had bricks and mortar, they had little liquidity. The mortgage payments were heavy, the house was expensive to maintain, and meanwhile, their pension provision had been significantly reduced compared to their ex-partner's.

The Longer-Term Risk

If all or most of your divorce settlement is tied up in the property, you may find:

- You are "asset rich but cash poor" with limited funds to cover day-to-day living.
- Your pension planning suffers, leaving you vulnerable in later life.
- You have reduced flexibility to make lifestyle choices, because all your wealth is locked in the house.

NOTE ON PENSIONS IN DIVORCE: Pensions can be worth as much, or more, than the family home. Don't overlook them when negotiating a settlement.

A Balanced Approach

The key isn't to automatically reject the home – it may well be the right choice for you and your children. But it's about considering the whole financial picture:

- Could you afford the running costs on your new single income?
- Are you sacrificing too much in terms of long-term pension provision?
- Would downsising free up cash and still provide security for your children?

Sometimes, letting go of the larger home and opting for a more manageable property can create the space, both financial and emotional, to rebuild your life with more freedom.

Remember: prioritising your children's stability doesn't just mean the physical house. It also means ensuring you are financially secure enough to support them into the future.

Protecting Yourself with Agreements

Conversations about prenuptial or postnuptial agreements can feel unromantic. But for women, especially those with children from previous relationships, businesses, or inherited assets, they provide clarity and protection. These legal agreements have increased in popularity over the years as our lives have become more complex.

To make them work:

- Both parties must have independent legal advice.
- Full financial disclosure is essential.
- Frame them not as mistrust, but as future-proofing your partnership.

Think of it as insurance: something you hope you never need, but invaluable if life takes an unexpected turn.

Reflection Exercise

- How do you currently structure money in your relationship?
- Do you feel financially independent as well as financially connected?
- If your relationship ended tomorrow, would you know your rights and financial position?

Take a moment to jot down your answers. Awareness is the first step to empowerment.

Closing Thoughts

Marriage and divorce both bring powerful emotions. Love can make us want to merge everything; separation can make us want to retreat from it all. But the goal isn't to lose yourself in either state, it's to maintain clarity, independence, and resilience while still embracing connection.

Because true partnership isn't about surrendering control. It's about standing side by side; strong, informed, and confident in both love and money.

Chapter 14 Workbook Exercises: Marriage, Divorce, and Your Money

1. **Quick Knowledge Check:** In my relationship, we:
   - ☐ Discuss money openly
   - ☐ Sometimes discuss money
   - ☐ Avoid money topics
   - ☐ I'm single

2. **One Key Reflection:** Our biggest financial challenge as a couple is:
   - ☐ Different money values
   - ☐ Income imbalance
   - ☐ Debt from past
   - ☐ Future goal alignment
   - ☐ Communication

3. **Priority Action This Week:**
   - ☐ Schedule a "money date" with my partner
   - ☐ Ensure I have my own bank account and credit history
   - ☐ List all joint and individual assets/debts

Chapter 15:
Widowhood – Navigating Financial Change

There are few life events that shake the ground beneath you as much as losing a life partner. The grief is raw and consuming, and yet at the very same time, practical matters come rushing in, often far sooner than you feel ready to face them.

If you are reading this because you've recently lost your partner, first take a breath. You don't have to do everything at once. You don't have to be "strong" every moment of every day. And you certainly don't have to navigate this alone.

Widowhood is not only an emotional transition, it's also, for many women, the first time they've carried full responsibility for the household's financial world. That shift can feel terrifying. I have seen women rise into strength they didn't know they had.

THE GRIEF FOG

Bereavement affects the hippocampus, the part of the brain responsible for memory and clear thinking. That's why many widows describe feeling "foggy." It's biology, not weakness. Understanding this can bring self-compassion: you don't need to rush big financial decisions during grief.

The First Days and Weeks: Focus on What Matters

In the immediate aftermath, there is so much pressure to "get everything sorted." But the truth is, very little needs to be decided instantly. In those first days and weeks, give yourself permission to do only what is essential.

First Week Priorities:

- **Death certificates** – You'll need multiple copies. Ask a friend or family member to help with these calls and paperwork.
- **Employer & pension providers** – Report the death to your partner's employer, pension, and insurance companies.
- **Access to funds** – If your partner managed the finances, you may need to locate bank accounts, cards, and key documents quickly. If possible, lean on a trusted ally to help here.

First Month Tasks:

- Notify banks, utilities, and credit cards. Be prepared that some joint accounts may freeze temporarily.
- Gather important paperwork: wills, property deeds, investments, insurance policies.
- Begin probate if necessary.

QUICK CHECK-IN: Who could be your "practical helper", a sibling, adult child, or close friend, so you don't carry every phone call and form on your own?

Understanding What Support is Available

This is a moment where knowing your entitlements can remove an additional stress.

State Benefits: If you are under State Pension age, you may qualify for Bereavement Support Payment. If you are over, you may inherit part of your partner's State Pension.

Workplace Benefits: Many employers offer a tax-free lump sum death-in-service benefit, or access to Employee Assistance Programmes for counselling and financial advice.

Insurance: Life cover or mortgage protection can ease immediate pressures. Don't hesitate to ask insurers or an adviser to walk you through the claims process step by step.

Taking Stock – When You're Ready

For some women, "taking stock" feels like a way of regaining control.
For others, even opening a bank statement feels unbearable.
Both responses are normal.

When the time feels right:

Make a financial inventory: assets, savings, property, and debts.

Understand Inheritance Tax: in most cases, assets left to a spouse are exempt. But knowing the position now can protect you later.

Create a snapshot of your position today, not because you need to make big decisions, but because clarity reduces anxiety.

The Big Decisions (That Can Wait)

Some choices, like where you live, or how to use inherited money, can feel urgent. In reality, they rarely are.

Housing: Staying in your current home may bring comfort, or it may feel like too much to carry emotionally or financially. Give yourself time. Downsizing can be empowering later, but don't rush. Unless the running costs are simply too high to service, this decision can be made in due course.

Investments & pensions: You may inherit pensions or investments. Hold them in savings if you need breathing room. There is no prize for making fast decisions in the fog of grief.

The Emotional Side of Money After Loss

Money and grief are deeply entwined. You may notice:

Hyper-caution: holding tightly to every penny.

Impulsivity: spending on distractions or to fill the void.

Guilt: finding it hard to spend on yourself.

All are normal. Awareness is the first step to balance. A financial coach may be a good place to start to help you work through your money emotions which can arise.

> **PRACTICAL TOOL:** The Pause Rule – Before any large financial decision, pause. Ask: *Am I doing this to ease pain, or because it genuinely serves my future?* If in doubt, wait.

Rebuilding – Creating a Life That Looks Different

When you are ready, you'll start to think about your future. This may feel daunting, your old plans may no longer fit. But this chapter of your life is also yours to write.

Reassess goals: Perhaps you want to travel, move closer to family, or invest in yourself. Let go of the idea that your goals must stay the same as before.

Build a support network: Financial advisers, bereavement groups, and money-savvy friends can all become anchors. You don't need to carry the load alone.

Find meaning in money: Many widows find comfort in supporting causes their partner loved, funding grandchildren's education, or simply allowing themselves joy in experiences they'd once postponed.

QUICK CHECK-IN: Write down one small financial decision that would bring you comfort or relief right now (e.g., setting up a direct debit, closing an unused account, or planning a short break). Circle it as your "first step."

Honouring Your Loved One

I often meet women who feel torn when it comes to changing the financial plans their partner once put in place. A phrase I hear often is: *"But my husband knew what he was doing, and he believed this was the right thing for us."*

That feeling is so deeply understandable. Your partner's choices were part of the life you built together. But here's the gentle truth: what was right for the two of you then, may not be right for you now. He planned for the life you shared; you are now navigating a life that looks very different.

Honouring your loved one doesn't mean keeping everything frozen in time. In fact, the most powerful way you can honour them is by shaping a financial strategy that serves you as you move forward; one that gives you stability, freedom, and even joy. Think of it as building upon the foundation they laid, but adapting it for the season you now find yourself in.

Give yourself permission to evolve. Choosing a path that supports your wellbeing is not a betrayal, it's an act of love, both for yourself and for the life you shared. With grace, forgiveness, and courage, you can create a financial plan that reflects who you are today, while still carrying the thread of the life you built together.

QUICK CHECK-IN: Is there one area of your finances you've left untouched because it feels "off limits"? Write it down now.

Looking Forward with Compassion

The pain of loss doesn't vanish, but it does evolve. Many women discover an unexpected resilience in widowhood, a new ability to take ownership, make decisions, and shape their financial lives with clarity and confidence.

There is no timeline for "moving on." This is not about replacing the past but about gently, gradually, creating a future that feels safe, purposeful, and uniquely yours.

Remember: widowhood changes your circumstances, but it does not diminish your strength.

Key Takeaways:

- Do only what's essential in the first weeks, everything else can wait.
- Seek support: financial, emotional, practical. You do not have to do this alone.
- Delay big decisions until you've had time to breathe.
- Allow yourself to spend on what nourishes you, self-care is not selfish.
- Rebuild at your own pace. A fulfilling new chapter is possible.

Journaling Exercise: A Conversation with Love

- Imagine sitting across the table from your partner.
- Write down what you think they would say to you now about your future.
- Ask yourself: *What would they most want for me? Security? Peace? Freedom to live fully?*
- Write a short letter back acknowledging their role in shaping your financial world, and giving yourself permission to adapt it to what you need now.

Keep this letter somewhere safe. On days when guilt creeps in, reread it. Let it remind you that building your own future is not walking away from your past, it's the truest way of honouring it.

Resources for Support

Practical and emotional support can be a lifeline at this stage. Here are some trusted places to start:

Rainbow Hunting (Emma Gray) – A grief coach who helps women find hope and colour again after loss. Emma's work blends compassion with practical guidance for life after bereavement.

Widowed and Young (WAY Foundation) – A UK charity offering peer-to-peer support for men and women under 50 who have lost a partner.

Cruse Bereavement Support – National UK organisation offering free counselling, helplines, and local groups.

At A Loss – Directory of bereavement support services across the UK, helping you connect with the right help for your situation.

Financial Advice for Bereaved Women – Many financial planners, including specialist advisers, offer services tailored to widows. Seek out someone who understands both the technical and emotional dimensions of this journey.

Chapter 15 Workbook Exercises: Widowhood – Navigating Financial Change

1. **Quick Knowledge Check:** If my partner died tomorrow, I would:
   - ☐ Know exactly what to do financially
   - ☐ Have some idea but need help
   - ☐ Feel completely lost
   - ☐ Prefer not to think about it

2. **One Key Reflection:** My biggest concern about managing finances alone would be:
   - ☐ Understanding investments
   - ☐ Dealing with paperwork
   - ☐ Making big decisions alone
   - ☐ Having enough money

3. **Priority Action This Week:**
   - ☐ Locate all important financial documents and passwords
   - ☐ Understand what benefits I might be entitled to
   - ☐ Identify a trusted person who could help with financial matters

Chapter 16:
Building Your Legacy

When we talk about legacy, most of us picture money being passed down through generations. But your true legacy is so much more than pounds and pence. It's the ripple of your values, the security you create, and the impact you leave on the people and causes that matter to you.

Legacy isn't only about what happens after we're gone. It's also about how we live now; the choices we make, the stories we tell, and the confidence we build in those around us. In this chapter, we'll explore not just the technical side of estate planning, but also the emotional and practical steps that help you shape a legacy that feels authentic, intentional, and deeply personal.

What Legacy Really Means (to us)

It's easy to picture legacy as grand estates and family fortunes. But for most of us, legacy looks like: the confidence we model; the stability we create; the causes we lift; the next generation we equip.

Our working definition: Legacy is the ongoing impact of our values, choices, relationships, and resources, before and after we're gone.

PAUSE & JOT: Which three words do you want people to associate with your legacy? (e.g., secure, generous, brave.)

Defining Our Legacy Vision

We don't have to wait until later life to plan this. In fact, the earlier we start, the more meaningful (and calm) everything feels, for us and for the people we love.

Try this quick start:

- Who/what matters? (people, places, causes)
- What do I want to protect or enable? (security, education, independence)
- What values do I want to embed? (learning, stewardship, compassion)

MINI-EXERCISE: Write a 2–3 sentence Legacy Intention.
For example, my legacy intention is "I want my legacy to create stability for my children, opportunities for my grandchildren through education, and ongoing support for women's financial education."

Values-Based Legacy Planning

Money carries our values further. It's not just about what we say matters to us, but how we show it through our choices. If you care deeply about education, generosity, or protecting the planet, your legacy can reflect those priorities through how you give, what you invest in, and the conversations you have with loved ones. A truly meaningful legacy connects money and meaning so that future generations can see your values lived out, not just listed.

What's one value you'd like your legacy to demonstrate (not just describe)?

Estate Planning Essentials

Estate planning isn't just for the wealthy or those later in life, it's for anyone who wants the reassurance that their wishes will be respected and their loved ones protected. Think of it as an act of love, a way to reduce uncertainty and potential stress for the people you care about most. Without even the basics in place, your family could face unnecessary delays, costs, and conflict at a time when they most need clarity and support.

Here are the essentials you need to know:

Will Writing

A will is the cornerstone of your estate plan. It's a legal document that sets out:

Who inherits your assets – from property and investments to sentimental items.

Who cares for minor children – without a will, the court makes this decision, not you.

Who manages your estate – your executor (the person you appoint) will handle everything from paying bills to distributing your assets.

Why it's important:

- Without a valid will, you are said to die intestate. This means the law decides who gets what according to rigid rules, regardless of your wishes or family dynamics.
- Partners who aren't married or in a civil partnership may be left with nothing, and disputes between relatives are sadly common.

Consequences of not having one:

- Loved ones may face delays accessing money they urgently need.
- The government decides how your estate is divided, which might not reflect your wishes.
- Family disagreements can arise, sometimes leading to expensive legal battles.

When and how to arrange one:
The best time to write a will is now. Life events such as marriage, divorce, buying a home, or having children should always prompt a review (and can invalidate previous wills, so be conscious of this). Wills can be drawn up through a solicitor (recommended for anything beyond the simplest circumstances), or you can create a straightforward version using an online service or will-writing company. Keep the original in a safe place and make sure your executors know where to find it.

Power of Attorney

A power of attorney is separate to your will and allows someone you trust to step in and make decisions if you're unable to. There are two main types in the UK:

Property and Financial Affairs Lasting Power of Attorney (LPA):
Covers financial decisions like paying bills, managing bank accounts, or even selling your home if needed.

Health and Welfare Lasting Power of Attorney (LPA): Covers decisions about your medical treatment, care, and where you live if you can't decide for yourself.

Why it's important:
Women statistically live longer than men, which means we're more likely to face periods of incapacity, whether through illness, accident, or simply longevity. Having powers of attorney in place ensures decisions are made by people you trust, not by strangers or the courts. I have heard many people refer to LPAs as being later life documents. But the unthinkable can happen to anyone at any time. So, I always advocate for having these documents in place, whatever your age.

Consequences of not having one:

- Your family may need to apply to the Court of Protection to manage your affairs, a lengthy, expensive, and stressful process.
- Until the court grants authority, no one can legally access your accounts or make health decisions for you, even your spouse or children.
- Important decisions may be delayed at a time when speed is critical.

One client I worked with relied on her husband's pension income as their primary household income. It had always been paid into his sole account. When he sadly suffered a stroke which left him incapacitated, she was unable to immediately access his account and their source of income. An LPA would have made this part of the process far less stressful had it been in place and she has since made sure to tell all her friends so they aren't faced with the same difficulties.

When and how to arrange one:
You can set up LPAs at any age (the earlier, the better). The forms are available online at **gov.uk**, and while you can complete them yourself, many people prefer to use a solicitor to ensure everything is correct. Once registered with the Office of the Public Guardian, they are legally valid and can be used immediately if needed.

Advance Directives (Living Wills)

An advance directive, also known as a living will, is a written statement of your preferences for medical treatment if you become unable to express them.

Why it's important:
These instructions give clarity to your loved ones and healthcare team, helping them make difficult choices with confidence that they're honouring your wishes. They also reduce the likelihood of family disputes at emotionally charged times.

Consequences of not having one:

- Family members may feel burdened with impossible decisions and potential guilt.
- Doctors may administer treatments you wouldn't have wanted.
- Disagreements between relatives can cause conflict and stress.

When and how to arrange one:
Advance directives can be drafted at any stage of life, and it's wise to review them regularly as your views or circumstances change. You don't need a solicitor to create one, though many people choose legal advice for peace of mind. The key is to ensure it's clearly written, signed, witnessed, and shared with your family and GP so that it's easily accessible if ever needed.

Bringing it together

These three documents, a will, powers of attorney, and advance directives, work hand in hand. Together, they create a strong foundation for your legacy planning and, perhaps more importantly, give you and your loved ones peace of mind. They don't need to be complicated or expensive, but they do need to be in place.

Estate Planning for Women's Unique Circumstances

Women face distinct estate planning challenges that generic advice often overlooks. Our longer lifespans mean we're more likely to outlive spouses and make financial decisions independently in later life. We're also more likely to be caregivers, which can complicate both our earning patterns and our estate planning needs.

Single Women's Estate Planning Priorities:

If you're single, whether by choice or circumstance, your estate planning is particularly crucial because you won't have a spouse to automatically inherit and manage your affairs. Consider who you trust to make decisions on your behalf and ensure they understand your values and wishes. I encourage single women who I work with to diversify their support network, appointing different people for different roles rather than burdening one person with everything.

When You're the Family Financial Manager:

As women we often become the de facto financial managers for our families, often inheriting this role when our parents age or our spouses become unable to manage their finances. If this describes you, then it will be important for you to address both your own wishes and the ongoing care of those who depend on you when you review your own estate planning. Consider creating detailed instructions for whoever will take over these responsibilities.

Blended Family Considerations:

Modern families often include children from previous relationships, creating complex inheritance situations. Often there is a desire to ensure that our children receive their intended inheritance, but the question around how this is facilitated whilst also providing for the surviving partner can become complicated. However, there are various options that can ensure everyone is provided for and protected. This might involve trusts, life insurance beneficiary planning, or other structures that protect everyone's interests and in this situation it is often beneficial to seek expert advice to ensure the planning is fit for purpose.

Advanced Estate Planning Strategies

As wealth grows, simple wills may not provide the flexibility or tax efficiency that many situations need. Advanced strategies (often with the assistance of professionals at this point) can help us maintain control while optimising the transfer of wealth to our beneficiaries.

Trust Structures for Different Goals:

Discretionary trusts offer flexibility when you're unsure about future circumstances. Trustees can adapt distributions based on beneficiaries' changing needs, protecting against beneficiaries' potential future financial difficulties or changes in tax law.

Life interest trusts can be particularly valuable in blended families, allowing the spouse to benefit from assets during their lifetime while ensuring the children ultimately inherit.

Bare trusts work well for straightforward gifts to adult children or grandchildren, offering tax advantages while maintaining simplicity.

Generation-Skipping Strategies:

If you have grandchildren, you might want to consider strategies that benefit them directly, while potentially reducing overall family tax burdens. Junior ISAs, pension contributions, and educational trusts can provide substantial long-term benefits while working within annual allowances.

Business Succession Planning:

Female entrepreneurs often overlook succession planning, but your business may be your most valuable asset. Whether you plan to pass it to family members, sell to employees, or exit to third parties, advance planning can optimise both financial returns and tax efficiency.

Tax-Efficient Legacy Planning

Understanding tax can make the difference between leaving behind a secure inheritance and leaving behind a headache. The rules around inheritance tax (IHT) can feel complicated, but once you know the basics, you can plan in a way that ensures more of your estate goes to the people and causes you care about, and less to the taxman.

Inheritance Tax (IHT)

In the UK, inheritance tax is charged at 40% on the value of estates above £325,000 (known as the nil rate band). Anything below this threshold is tax-free.

Spouses and civil partners: Anything you leave to your spouse or civil partner is usually exempt from inheritance tax, no matter the amount. Plus, any unused portion of your nil rate band can be transferred to them, effectively doubling the allowance for couples.

The Residence Nil Rate Band: In addition to the £325,000 allowance, you can pass on an extra £175,000 if you're leaving your main home to direct descendants such as children or grandchildren. Together, this means a couple could potentially pass on up to £1 million before IHT applies.

Who doesn't count as a direct descendant: It's worth noting that this additional allowance doesn't apply to siblings, cousins, aunts, or uncles, even if they're very close to you.

What happens if you don't plan: Without taking advantage of these allowances, your estate could face a 40% tax bill on anything above the threshold. For many families, this can mean a significant portion of hard-earned wealth being lost unnecessarily.

Note on Estate Value: When calculating inheritance tax, HMRC looks at the net value of your estate. This means mortgages and certain debts are deducted from the total before tax is applied. For example, a £1 million home with a £400,000 mortgage would be valued at £600,000 for IHT purposes.

The allowances we've outlined here are the main ones most families use. In reality, the calculation can also take into account factors like lifetime gifts, business or agricultural relief, and charitable legacies. This is why tailored advice can make such a big difference.

Gifting Strategies

Making gifts during your lifetime can reduce the size of your estate and, in turn, reduce your future inheritance tax liability.

Annual Exemption: You can give away £3,000 per year (in total, not per person) without it counting towards your estate. If you didn't use last year's allowance, you can carry it forward once, so potentially £6,000 in a single year.

Small Gifts: You can also make small gifts of up to £250 per person, per year to as many people as you like, as long as they don't also receive part of your £3,000 exemption.

Wedding and Civil Partnership Gifts: You can give up to £5,000 to a child, £2,500 to a grandchild, or £1,000 to anyone else for their wedding or civil partnership, inheritance tax-free.

Potentially Exempt Transfers (PETs): Larger gifts can also be made, and if you survive for seven years after making them, they fall outside your estate completely. If you die within seven years, taper relief may reduce the tax due after three years.

Gifts out of income: If you have surplus income after covering your living expenses, you can make regular gifts (for example, paying school fees for grandchildren) which are immediately free from inheritance tax, regardless of when you die.

Key tip: With any of these allowances, the key is to document everything carefully. HMRC will expect evidence to support your estate's claim for IHT relief, and without records, your executors may face challenges. Keep notes of when gifts were made, how much they were for, and whether they came from capital or surplus income.

You can use HMRC's form IHT403 – Gifts and Other Transfers of Value (available on gov.uk) to record this information. Completing it as you go makes life much easier for your executors later and helps ensure the reliefs you're entitled to aren't lost.

What happens if you don't plan: If you leave gifting too late or don't structure it carefully, your estate may end up paying inheritance tax on amounts that could have been passed on tax-free. Families often miss out simply because they weren't aware of the rules.

NOTE ON GIFTS: You can give away up to £3,000 each tax year inheritance-tax free (your "annual exemption"). Larger gifts may be tax-free if you live for 7 years after making them.

Charitable Giving

Charitable giving is not only a powerful way to support the causes you care about, it can also reduce your inheritance tax bill.

Tax-free status: Any gifts left to charity in your will are entirely free from inheritance tax.

Reduced tax rate: If you leave at least 10% of your net estate to charity, the inheritance tax rate on the remainder drops from 40% to 36%. This can make a significant difference to both your chosen charity and your beneficiaries.

Lifetime giving: Charitable donations made while you're alive can also reduce your income tax bill, as higher- and additional-rate taxpayers can claim back tax relief on donations made through Gift Aid and donations fall immediately outside of your estate for inheritance tax purposes.

What happens if you don't plan: Your estate may pay more tax than necessary, and your ability to support the charities and causes that matter to you could be reduced. By planning ahead, you can often benefit both your loved ones and the organisations you care about.

Bringing it all together

Tax rules may feel dry, but they carry real weight in shaping your legacy. By making use of allowances, gifting strategically, and considering charitable giving, you can dramatically reduce the tax burden on your estate. More importantly, you'll know that your wealth is working in line with your values, supporting your family and your chosen causes, rather than being unnecessarily eroded.

Providing for Children and Grandchildren

For many women, one of the most meaningful aspects of legacy planning isn't just about passing on money it's about supporting the next generation (remember the wisdom years elephants?!) and giving them the tools to thrive. Whether that's helping with education, providing a financial springboard, or knowing your children and grandchildren will always feel secure, this often sits right at the heart of women's legacy planning.

This isn't only about wealth transfer; it's about weaving your values into the lives of those who follow you. Women often carry the responsibility of nurturing, teaching, and guiding within families and legacy planning is a natural extension of that role. By combining financial support with financial education, you can pass on both resources and resilience.

Education Funding

Education is one of the most common ways women choose to support the next generation.

Junior ISAs and children's pensions are powerful tools. They grow tax-free and can give children a life-changing head start. A modest contribution made early can compound into something significant by adulthood.

Consider the rules around when the individual can access the funds and how they should be invested for the length of time they will be held for. Each will carry its own rules which you will need to carefully consider.

Paying school fees or university costs directly is another effective strategy. These payments count as exempt gifts for inheritance tax purposes, which means you can reduce your taxable estate while supporting your children or grandchildren when they need it most.

Think of it this way: you're not just paying for qualifications, you're investing in confidence, opportunities, and independence for their future.

Teaching Financial Values

Money without guidance can easily overwhelm. Over the years I've seen a striking difference between families who simply inherit money and those who inherit wealth. Money is a lump sum, a figure on a statement. It can be spent quickly, mismanaged, or even become a source of conflict. Wealth, on the other hand, is money combined with meaning: the knowledge of how to use it, the values that shape decisions, and the confidence to steward it well. When financial wisdom is passed down alongside financial resources, the gift doesn't just preserve its value, it grows, supports, and empowers the next generation. That is the true difference: money is a transaction; wealth is a legacy.

Here are some practical ideas to help you pass on wealth beyond money:

- Host a family money meeting once a year. This could be as simple as sharing what you've learned about budgeting or investing, and encouraging younger family members to ask questions.
- Consider linking a gift (for example, funding a Junior ISA) to a money lesson such as showing a child how compound growth works over time.
- Some families even include "money milestones" in their legacy plans: for example, children receive a gift when they complete a financial education course, or once they've saved a set amount themselves.

Trusts for Protection

Trusts can sound technical, but at their heart they are simply a legal arrangement that allows you to set aside assets for someone else's benefit, with rules about how and when they can be accessed. For women who want to balance generosity with guidance, trusts can be a powerful part of legacy planning.

They are particularly useful if you:

- Want to protect assets until beneficiaries reach a certain age or milestone.
- Prefer gifts to be distributed gradually rather than as a single lump sum.
- Have concerns about a child's or grandchild's ability to manage money wisely (whether because of age, experience, or vulnerability).
- Want reassurance that wealth will be used in line with your values. For example, funding education, a first home, or health needs, or protected from a beneficiary's potential future divorce.

Why Trusts Matter

Passing on wealth outright can sometimes create challenges. Young adults may not yet have the maturity to manage large sums, and even older beneficiaries may be vulnerable to pressure from others, divorce settlements, or financial missteps. A trust adds a protective layer ensuring your gift is available, but stewarded in a way that safeguards both the money and your loved one's wellbeing.

Trusts can also help preserve wealth across generations. Instead of being swallowed up in one go, assets can be distributed steadily and with purpose, keeping your legacy alive over many years.

Types of Trusts You Might Encounter

There are different kinds of trust, but here are some of the most common in a family legacy context:

Bare Trusts – Simple trusts often used for children. The assets belong to the child outright, but a trustee manages them until the child reaches 18 (16 in Scotland). At that point, they gain full control.

Discretionary Trusts – These give trustees the power to decide how and when beneficiaries receive money. They're useful if you want flexibility, or if circumstances may change (for example, one grandchild may need more support than another).

Interest in Possession Trusts – A beneficiary has the right to income from the trust (such as rent from a property) during their lifetime, but the capital is preserved for others (often the next generation).

Trusts for Vulnerable Beneficiaries – Specifically designed for beneficiaries who are disabled or otherwise vulnerable, these trusts offer extra protections and can have favourable tax treatment.

You don't need to know every detail of these – the key takeaway is that there is likely to be a trust structure that fits your circumstances. A solicitor or financial planner, like Eva Wealth, can advise on the most appropriate type.

The Tax Angle

Trusts can be tax-efficient, but the rules are complex and it's important to seek advice before setting one up. In the UK:

- Some trusts are treated as Potentially Exempt Transfers (like outright gifts) and fall outside your estate if you survive seven years.
- Others may be subject to periodic charges (up to 6% every 10 years) or exit charges when assets are distributed.
- Certain trusts designed for vulnerable or disabled beneficiaries can receive special tax advantages.

The right trust, correctly structured, can protect wealth and reduce inheritance tax exposure, but the wrong set-up can create unnecessary costs, so professional guidance is essential.

Putting a Trust in Place

When to consider one: Trusts are particularly valuable once you have accumulated significant assets, or if you know you want to earmark funds for specific purposes.

How to arrange one: Trusts must be created formally, usually through a solicitor or estate planning professional. You'll need to:

- Decide what assets to place in the trust.
- Appoint trustees (people or professionals you deeply trust to manage the assets responsibly).
- Define the rules – who benefits, how, and when.

Choose trustees carefully. They carry both legal responsibility and moral weight in ensuring your wishes are honoured. Many people choose a mix of family members and professional trustees to balance personal insight with technical expertise.

Trusts in Practice

Imagine you want to leave £200,000 to your two grandchildren. Rather than passing it outright at 18, you set up a discretionary trust. The trustees are instructed to use the funds to help with university costs, first homes, or setting up a business, but not to release it all at once. This way, the money supports their opportunities without overwhelming them, and the capital can still be safeguarded if one of them goes through a divorce or financial difficulty.

In summary, trusts provide a way to give generously while still offering protection, guidance, and structure. They can turn financial support into a lasting legacy – one that reflects not just your wealth, but your care and foresight for generations to come.

TRUSTS AT A GLANCE

Bare Trust – Assets belong to the child outright, but a trustee manages them until age 18 (16 in Scotland). Simple and straightforward.

Discretionary Trust – Trustees decide how and when to distribute money. Flexible, good for changing circumstances or unequal needs.

Interest in Possession Trust – One person receives income from the assets (e.g., rent or dividends), while the capital is preserved for others later.

Trusts for Vulnerable Beneficiaries – Designed for disabled or vulnerable individuals, offering extra protections and favourable tax treatment.

There's no "one-size-fits-all" trust. The right structure(s) depends on your family's needs, values, and the legacy you want to create.
If you are considering Trusts as part of your legacy planning, speak to a professional adviser to make sure that you get it right.

Bringing it together

Providing for children and grandchildren is about more than money. It's about equipping them with both resources and responsibility, security and self-belief. By blending financial tools with conversations and teaching, you leave not just wealth, but wisdom. That combination is one of the most powerful legacies you can create.

Supporting Causes You Care About

Charitable giving can be one of the most powerful and fulfilling parts of your legacy. For many women, it's not only about leaving financial security for family, it's also about using resources to make a difference in the wider world. This could mean supporting a cause that has shaped your life, championing issues you're passionate about, or simply giving back to your local community.

There are many ways to structure charitable giving as part of your estate plan:

Leave a gift directly in your will to a charity you care about. This could be a specific sum, a percentage of your estate, or even a valuable item such as artwork, jewellery, or property.

Set up a charitable trust or foundation if you want your giving to continue long after you're gone, with trustees overseeing how funds are distributed. This can be particularly meaningful if you want your family to remain involved in directing your legacy.

Use a donor-advised fund (DAF): Organisations such as the Charities Aid Foundation (CAF) in the UK allow you to make tax-deductible contributions into a central fund during your lifetime. You then have the flexibility to decide later which charities or projects to support. This can be especially helpful if you want to act now for tax efficiency but aren't yet certain which causes to prioritise.

If you're unsure which specific charities to support, consider focusing on themes that matter to you – education, health, the environment, or women's empowerment and then directing funds through organisations like CAF or even local community foundations. They can ensure your money is used effectively while still giving you choice and flexibility.

Charitable giving also comes with valuable tax benefits:

- Any gift to charity is inheritance tax-free.
- If you leave 10% or more of your estate to charity, the inheritance tax rate on the remainder of your estate falls from 40% to 36%.
- Lifetime giving (through Gift Aid) can also reduce your income tax bill, adding another layer of benefit.

Bringing it together:
Supporting causes you care about allows your legacy to reach beyond your family and into the wider world. Whether through a carefully chosen charity, a donor-advised fund, or a local community project, this part of your plan can reflect your deepest values and create a ripple effect long after you're gone.

LEGACY PLANNING ACROSS LIFE STAGES

Your legacy plan will evolve as your life does; it's unlikely to be a one-hit, all done piece of work. For most of us, the following approach will provide a helpful framework:

Early Career: A simple will, power of attorney, and basic protection.

Mid-Career: Consider trusts, beneficiary updates, and tax planning.

Pre-Retirement: Time to fine-tune, often the stage where larger charitable gifts are made.

Retirement: Begin putting plans into action through gifts, philanthropy, and family support.

Family Wealth Conversations

One of the most important aspects of legacy planning is communication. Many families avoid discussing money and inheritance, but these conversations can prevent confusion and conflict later.

Begin with your values and goals rather than specific pound amounts. Explain why you're making certain decisions and what you hope to achieve. This helps loved ones understand your thinking and reduces the risk of misinterpretation.

It's also important to recognise that one of the most overlooked parts of estate planning isn't the paperwork, it's the conversations. Wills and legacy decisions made in silence can leave families shocked or hurt, especially when grief is already raw. Children or relatives may not understand why you've chosen to divide your estate in a certain way, and without context, assumptions and resentment can quickly grow. Talking openly about your wishes while you're alive, even if it feels uncomfortable, can prevent disputes, reduce confusion, and allow your loved ones to feel included in the process. These conversations don't have to involve every detail of your estate, but sharing the why behind your decisions provides clarity, peace, and the chance for your family to focus on remembering you rather than questioning your intentions.

Consider involving adult children in your planning process. This doesn't mean you need to disclose everything, but offering some insight into your values and intentions can help them feel informed and respected. And if the thought of leading these conversations feels daunting, working with a financial planner can help facilitate them in a supportive and neutral way.

Updating Your Legacy Plan

Life changes, and so should your plan. Review it every 3–5 years, and always after big life events. Keep beneficiary forms up to date, these can override your will.

The Emotional Side of Legacy Planning

In the conversations I've had with women, the theme of guilt is something that has emerged time and again. Worry, or even conflict about your wealth is also not unusual. Remember, building something to pass on is an act of love. Be clear about your intentions, manage expectations, and seek support if emotions feel overwhelming.

Your Living Legacy

Finally, consider that legacy isn't only about what happens after you're gone, it's about how you live now. Mentoring, volunteering, supporting causes, and modelling financial confidence are all part of your living legacy. Your legacy doesn't have to look like anyone else's. What matters is that it reflects your values, supports the people and causes you care about, and gives you peace of mind.

YOUR LEGACY PLANNING TIMELINE: A SIMPLE CHECKLIST

In Your 30s:

- Write your first will (especially if you have children)
- Review life insurance needs
- Begin conversations with your partner about wishes
- Consider guardianship for minor children

In Your 40s–50s:

- Review and update your will
- Set up Lasting Powers of Attorney
- Start specific legacy planning (who gets what)
- Have honest conversations with adult children about inheritance plans

In Your 60s+:

- Review everything every 2–3 years
- Ensure executors still want the role

- Update your letter of wishes with specific sentimental items
- Consider tax-efficient gifting strategies
- Share your wishes clearly with family

After Major Life Events (any age):

- Review immediately after: marriage, divorce, birth of children/grandchildren, death of beneficiary, significant wealth changes.

Life transitions are inevitable, but they don't have to throw you off course. Whether you're climbing the career ladder, navigating a relationship change, dealing with loss, or planning your legacy, each stage offers an opportunity to pause, reassess and strengthen your financial foundation.

The secret isn't just in strategies, it's in cultivating the confidence to adapt. You are more resilient than you realise. With the right tools and mindset, you can meet financial change with wisdom and grace.

And please remember: seeking help is never weakness, it's strength. Whether from professionals, trusted friends, or a supportive community, asking for guidance is one of the smartest financial decisions you can make.

Your financial journey is uniquely yours. Every transition is a stepping stone towards aligning your money more closely with your values and your vision for life. Embrace these changes, trust yourself, and know that you have everything you need to create the financial future you desire.

Chapter 16 Workbook Exercises: Building Your Legacy

1. **Quick Knowledge Check:** I currently have:
   - ☐ An up-to-date will
   - ☐ Powers of attorney in place
   - ☐ Beneficiaries named on pensions
   - ☐ None of these
   - ☐ Some but not all

2. **One Key Reflection:** When I think about my legacy, I want to be remembered for:

3. **Priority Action This Week:**
   - ☐ Make an appointment to update or create my will
   - ☐ Check beneficiary details on all accounts and pensions
   - ☐ Have a conversation with family about my wishes

Remember, your legacy doesn't need to be perfect or grand. What matters is that it reflects who you are, what you value, and the love and care you want to pass on.

Part 5: Taking Action

"You may be the first generation of women to do it differently - don't be afraid to begin." - Michelle Obama

You've learned about understanding your money story, mastering essential financial management, growing your wealth, and navigating life's transitions. Now comes the most important part: taking action. Knowledge without action is just potential energy, it's the doing that transforms your financial life.

This final section is your roadmap from knowledge to action. I'll help you create a personalised financial plan, guide you in working with professionals when needed, explore how sharing your knowledge can deepen your own understanding, and celebrate the journey toward your financial freedom.

Remember, you don't have to be perfect to start, and you don't have to do everything at once. Small, consistent actions compound into extraordinary results over time. Your future self is counting on the decisions you make today.

Chapter 17:
Creating Your Financial Plan

Humans consistently underestimate how long tasks will take and how much they'll cost. You budget £800 for new carpets. The quote comes in at £1,100. You plan to save £5,000 in a year, but eighteen months later you're only at £3,200. You allocate three months for a home project that takes five. Sound familiar? This is the 'planning fallacy' – our universal human tendency to underestimate how long things take and what they'll cost. It's not a personal failing; it's a cognitive bias we all share. The solution is beautifully simple: build in a buffer. Add 20–30% to your financial timelines and cost estimates as standard practice. Yes, your optimistic brain will insist you're being overly cautious. But your future self, the one who actually achieves goals on schedule without financial stress, will be immensely grateful you planned for reality instead of best-case scenarios.

This buffer mindset is foundational to creating a financial plan that actually works. Because a good financial plan isn't built on best-case scenarios and perfect execution – it's built on realistic expectations and room for life to happen. Which is exactly what we're going to create together in this chapter.

Your Personal Financial Blueprint

A financial plan isn't a rigid document that sits in a drawer gathering dust, it's a living, breathing guide that evolves with your life. Think of it as your personal GPS for money decisions, helping you navigate toward your goals while allowing for detours and discoveries along the way.

The beauty of creating your own financial plan is that it reflects your unique circumstances, values, and dreams. No one else has exactly your combination of goals, challenges, and opportunities, which is why a personalised approach is so powerful.

And unlike that optimistic carpet budget or overly ambitious savings timeline, this plan is going to be grounded in reality (your reality), with built-in flexibility for when things don't go exactly to plan. Because they won't. And that's okay.

Getting Started: The Foundation

Before diving into strategies, it is important to establish your financial foundation. This groundwork will support everything else you build.

Your Financial Snapshot:

Begin by taking an honest look at where you stand today. This isn't about judgment, it's about clarity. You can't plan a journey without knowing your starting point.

List your assets: savings accounts, investments, property, pensions, and any other valuable possessions. Don't forget to include the value of items like jewellery or art if they're significant.

Next, document your liabilities: mortgages, credit card debt, student loans, and any money you owe to family or friends. Be thorough and honest, this information is for you, not anyone else.

Calculate your net worth by subtracting your total liabilities from your total assets. Whether this number is positive or negative, it's simply your starting point. Every wealthy person started somewhere, and many started with negative net worth.

Assets (what you own)	
Cash / Savings Accounts	£
Investments (stocks, ISAs, funds)	£
Property (home, rental, land)	£
Pensions (workplace & personal)	£
Valuable possessions (e.g., jewellery, art)	£
Other assets	£
Total Assets	**£**
Liabilities (what you owe)	
Mortgage(s)	£
Credit Card Debt	£
Student Loans	£
Car Loans	£
Money owed to family/friends	£
Other debts	£
Total Liabilities	**£**

Net Worth = Total Assets – Total Liabilities = £ ____________________

QUICK CHECK-IN: How does this number make you feel, relieved, motivated, surprised, or perhaps a mix?

Cash Flow Analysis:

Understanding your monthly cash flow is crucial for financial planning. Track your income from all sources, then list your expenses in categories: housing, food, transportation, entertainment, and savings.

Use this analysis to identify opportunities. Where can you reduce expenses without significantly impacting your quality of life? Where can you potentially increase income? What percentage of your income are you currently saving?

WORKSHEET: CASH FLOW ANALYSIS

Track your monthly income and expenses to see where your money is going. This will give you clarity on opportunities to adjust and align with your goals.

Income (monthly)	
Salary / Wages	£
Bonuses / Overtime	£
Business / Freelance Income	£
Investment Income (dividends, interest, rent)	£
Other Income (child benefit, gifts, etc.)	£
Total Monthly Income	**£**
Expenses (monthly)	
Housing (rent / mortgage, council tax, utilities	£
Food & Groceries	£
Transportation (car, fuel, public transport)	£
Insurance (life, home, health, car, etc.)	£
Debt Payments (credit cards, loans)	£
Savings & Investments	£

Lifestyle & Entertainment (eating out, holidays, subscriptions)	£
Miscellaneous	£
Total Monthly Expenses	**£**

Quick Calculations

- Net Monthly Position (Income – Expenses): £ ______________________
- Savings Rate (Savings ÷ Income x 100): __________ %

QUICK CHECK-IN – REFLECTION PROMPTS:

- Where could I reduce spending without it impacting my quality of life?
- Where could I potentially increase income?
- How do I feel about the percentage of my income I'm currently saving?

Setting Your Financial Goals

Goals give your money purpose and your plan direction. Without clear goals, it's easy to drift financially, never quite achieving the life you want.

The Three Horizons:

Structure your goals across three time horizons to create a balanced approach:

Short-term goals (1–2 years): These might include building an emergency fund, paying off credit card debt, or saving for a holiday. These goals provide quick wins that build momentum and confidence.

Medium-term goals (3–10 years): Consider goals like buying a home, changing careers, or building a substantial investment portfolio. These goals require more planning and consistent effort but are still concrete and achievable.

Long-term goals (10+ years): Think about retirement, financial independence, or legacy planning. These goals might seem distant, but starting early gives you the powerful advantage of compound growth.

Making Goals Specific and Meaningful:
Instead of "save more money," try "save £200 per month for a £5,000 emergency fund within 25 months." Specific goals are easier to plan for and more motivating to pursue.

Connect each financial goal to a deeper why. Saving for retirement isn't just about having money, it might be about having the freedom to travel, volunteer, or spend time with grandchildren. Understanding your deeper motivations helps maintain commitment when the journey gets challenging.

WORKBOOK ENTRY: SETTING YOUR FINANCIAL GOALS
Your goals give your money direction and purpose. Use the table below to map out your short, medium, and long-term goals. Make them **specific** and connect them to your deeper **why.**

Time Horizon	My Goal (specific + measurable)	Why This Matters to Me	Target Date	First Step I Can Take
Short-Term (1–2 years)	e.g., Save £200 per month to build a £5,000 emergency fund	To feel secure and reduce anxiety	Dec 2026	Open a new savings account
Medium-Term (3–10 years)	e.g., Save £20,000 for a house deposit	To create stability and build equity	2030	Research mortgage options
Long-Term (10+ years)	e.g., Build pension fund of £500,000	To retire early and travel freely	2045	Increase monthly pension contributions

QUICK CHECK-IN – REFLECTION PROMPTS:

- Which of these goals feels the most exciting right now?
- Which one feels the most challenging? Why?
- What support, habits, or systems might help me stay committed when it gets tough?

Creating Your Action Plan

With your foundation established and goals defined, it's time to create your step-by-step action plan.

Prioritising Your Goals: You probably have more goals than you can tackle simultaneously, and that's normal. Prioritise based on urgency, impact, and personal importance.

Generally, focus on high-interest debt elimination and emergency fund building before investing for growth. However, if your employer offers pension matching, contribute enough to get the full match even while paying off debt, it's free money you can't afford to leave on the table.

The Monthly Money Plan: Create a monthly financial routine that moves you steadily toward your goals. This might include:

- Automatic transfers to savings and investment accounts
- Regular debt payments above the minimum
- Monthly budget reviews and adjustments
- Quarterly goal progress assessments

Building in Flexibility: Life rarely goes according to plan, so build flexibility into your financial plan. Create contingency strategies for different scenarios. What if you lose your job? What if you receive an unexpected windfall? What if your goals change?

Tracking and Adjusting: A financial plan without regular review and adjustment is just a well-intentioned document. Schedule regular check-ins to assess your progress and make necessary adjustments.

Monthly or Quarterly Reviews: Each month, review your spending against your budget, assess progress toward goals, and identify any needed adjustments. This doesn't need to be a lengthy process; 30 minutes can be sufficient.

Quarterly Deep Dives: Every three months, conduct a more thorough review.

Annual Overhauls: Once a year, completely review and update your financial plan. Make sure you assess your investment performance, review insurance coverage, and consider whether your goals or priorities have shifted.

Situational Reviews: When there has been a significant change in your circumstances have a deep dive review. This is when you might make significant strategy changes, update your will, or adjust your investment allocation.

Common Planning Pitfalls

You're not the first person to create a financial plan, and you won't be the first to encounter obstacles along the way. The mistakes that derail financial plans are remarkably consistent across different people, incomes, and circumstances. Knowing what they are means you can spot them coming and avoid them entirely. Watch out for these common pitfalls.

Perfectionism Paralysis: Don't wait until you have the perfect plan to start. A good plan implemented is better than a perfect plan that never gets started.

All-or-Nothing Thinking: If you miss a savings goal one month, don't abandon the entire plan. Financial planning is about progress, not perfection.

Comparing to Others: Your plan should reflect your values and circumstances, not someone else's. Avoid the trap of thinking you're behind because your plan looks different from a friend's or colleague's.

Ignoring Inflation: When setting long-term goals, consider how inflation might affect your purchasing power. A goal that seems adequate today might fall short in 20 years.

Technology and Tools

Leverage technology to make financial planning easier and more effective. Budgeting apps can automate expense tracking, investment platforms can handle portfolio rebalancing, and calendar reminders can ensure you don't miss important financial tasks.

However, don't let technology overwhelm you. Choose tools that simplify your life rather than complicate it. The best financial plan is one you'll actually follow, regardless of how sophisticated the tools involved.

At Eva Wealth we have built MyWealthVault to give you the tools to do just that. As a digital portal you can keep your plan as updated as frequently as life changes, track your goals and have access to courses and updated content to make sure you feel in the know at all times.

Chapter 17 Workbook Exercises: Creating Your Financial Plan

1. **Quick Knowledge Check:** My current financial plan is:
   - ☐ Comprehensive and written down
   - ☐ Mostly in my head
   - ☐ Basic but needs work
   - ☐ Non-existent

2. **One Key Reflection:** My biggest obstacle to financial planning is:
   - ☐ Don't know where to start
   - ☐ Too overwhelming
   - ☐ Keeps changing
   - ☐ Need professional help

3. **Priority Action This Week:**
   - ☐ Write down my top 3 financial goals with target dates
   - ☐ Calculate my current net worth
   - ☐ Schedule monthly money review dates for the next 3 months

Chapter 18:
Working with Financial Professionals

Financial planning can sometimes feel like trying to piece together a 1,000-piece puzzle without the picture on the box. There's no shame in seeking professional guidance, in fact, knowing when to ask for help is a sign of financial wisdom, not weakness.

You might benefit from professional help if you're:

- Facing a major life transition like divorce, retirement, or bereavement.
- Dealing with complex financial arrangements (multiple properties, business ownership, inheritance).
- Feeling overwhelmed by investment choices and jargon.
- Simply wanting objective guidance from someone with the expertise and emotional distance to help you see clearly.

I've had so many women say to me, *"I feel like I should be able to manage this myself"*. Please hear me on this, getting professional support is not failure. It's often the most efficient and empowering way to move forward.

Types of Financial Professionals

The financial services industry can feel like a maze, different titles, qualifications, and fee models. Understanding who does what will help you choose the right professional for you.

Independent Financial Advisers (IFAs)

- IFAs provide comprehensive financial planning and can recommend products from across the market (as opposed to a 'restricted adviser' who can only advise from their company's range of products).

- They are required to act in your best interests and must clearly disclose how they're compensated.
- They can help with retirement planning, investments, insurance, and tax planning.

Chartered Financial Planners

- These advisers have additional qualifications and tend to focus on holistic, long-term financial strategies.
- They're often ideal if you want a broad plan that integrates all aspects of your financial life.

Specialist Advisers

- Some advisers specialise in pensions, inheritance tax, investments, or mortgages.
- If you have a very specific need, a specialist may be the best fit.

Fee-Only vs. Commission-Based

- Fee-only advisers charge you directly for their advice (hourly, flat fee, or a % of assets).
- Commission-based advisers earn from the products they recommend. While not automatically bad, this can create conflicts of interest, so always ask questions.
- In the UK the Retail Distribution Review in 2012 removed commission from pensions and investments, so today any payment to a financial adviser should carry an explicit fee agreement between you and them.
- The right adviser will never make you feel silly for asking how they're paid. If you sense discomfort or vagueness around this, that's a red flag.

Finding the Right Adviser

Choosing an adviser is like choosing a personal trainer, lawyer, or doctor, you want someone qualified, trustworthy, and aligned with your values.

Research & Credentials: Make sure they're regulated by the Financial Conduct Authority (FCA). You can check the FCA register online. Look for additional qualifications like Chartered status, or memberships in professional bodies.

The Interview Process: Most advisers offer a free initial meeting. Use this as a chance to check fit, not just technical skills. Ask about their typical clients, their investment philosophy, their communication style. Pay attention to whether you feel listened to and respected.

Questions to Ask:

- How are you compensated, and what conflicts of interest could exist?
- What's your investment philosophy and approach to risk?
- How do you usually communicate with clients, and how often?
- Can you give me references from clients like me?
- What happens if you're not available or retire?

Avoid advisers who:

- Guarantee returns (nobody can).
- Pressure you into quick decisions.
- Can't clearly explain their fees.
- Make you feel rushed, judged, or inadequate.

Remember, if an adviser makes you feel belittled, it says everything about them, and nothing about you.

Making the Relationship Work

A successful relationship with a financial professional is a partnership. Here's how to get the most from it:

Be Honest and Complete: Share the full picture, debts, fears, even messy money habits. An adviser can only help if they understand the real situation.

Communicate Your Goals and Values: Say what matters to you: whether that's ethical investing, early retirement, or simply sleeping better at night.

Stay Engaged: Don't hand everything over and check out. Ask questions, learn, and stay in the loop.

Review Regularly: Life changes, your financial plan should too. Annual reviews are the bare minimum. Establish how you are going to stay engaged ongoing.

Alternative Professional Support

Sometimes you don't need a full financial planner but still need specific advice. At different points you may find that the following professionals are the right people to turn to:

- **Accountants** for tax planning and filing.
- **Solicitors** for wills, trusts, and estate planning.
- **Mortgage brokers** for finding the best deal.
- **Insurance brokers** for making sure your family is protected.

If you decide to work with a financial planner, chances are you'll also need one or more of these professionals at some stage. A good planner doesn't just give advice in isolation, they often act like the conductor of your financial orchestra. They coordinate with your accountant, solicitor, or broker, staying connected to what each is doing so they can keep a complete picture of your finances and help you get the very best out of everything.

The Cost-Benefit Analysis

Yes, professional advice costs money, typically £150–£300 per hour for specific guidance, or around 0.5–1% of assets under management annually for ongoing advice. But whether this cost makes sense depends largely on the complexity of your situation.

When professional advice often pays for itself:

Boost your investment returns: even a 0.5% improvement in returns through better portfolio construction or asset allocation can outweigh advice fees, especially over decades.

Save you thousands in tax: a financial planner might spot inheritance tax planning opportunities, pension contribution strategies, or capital gains tax efficiencies you'd miss, potentially saving £5,000–£50,000+ depending on your circumstances.

Protect you from catastrophic risks: identifying gaps in protection (life insurance, income protection, wills, lasting powers of attorney) before you need them can be literally priceless.

Avoid costly mistakes: withdrawing from pensions incorrectly, missing allowances, or poor timing on major decisions can cost far more than advice fees.

Free up your time and reduce stress: if financial decisions are keeping you up at night or consuming hours of research, professional guidance might be worth it for peace of mind alone.

Navigate major life transitions: divorce, inheritance, redundancy, selling a business, or retirement are moments when expert guidance can be transformational.

Coordinate complex moving parts: when you have multiple pensions, investment accounts, properties, and tax considerations, a professional can see the full picture in ways you might not.

Complexity matters more than wealth. You might have £500,000 and need minimal advice (simple situation, long time horizon, comfortable with DIY investing), or £100,000 and desperately need professional guidance (divorce settlement, disabled dependent, self-employment with variable income). The question isn't "Am I wealthy enough for advice?" but rather "Is my situation complex enough that professional expertise would add meaningful value?".

Signs your situation might benefit from professional advice:

- Multiple income sources or self-employment
- Significant assets across different account types (pensions, ISAs, investments, property)
- Complex family situations (blended families, dependents with special needs, elderly parents)
- Major life transitions on the horizon
- Inheritance planning or intergenerational wealth transfer
- You're approaching retirement with various pension pots
- Tax implications you don't fully understand
- You're consistently avoiding financial decisions due to overwhelm

Even if you prefer managing things yourself, an occasional second opinion can be invaluable, particularly at major life junctures or when making irreversible decisions like pension withdrawals. Think of it as hiring an editor for a manuscript you've written: they're not taking over your work, but they might spot gaps, opportunities, or risks you've overlooked.

The key is finding the right level of advice for your situation: perhaps that's a one-off review, an annual check-in, or full ongoing financial planning. Not everyone needs comprehensive advice, but almost everyone benefits from it at certain points in their financial life.

Working with Online Services

Technology has opened up new options for financial advice, robo-advisers, online platforms, and hybrid services.

- These can be great if your situation is straightforward and you're cost-conscious.
- But for complex finances or big life transitions, nothing replaces tailored, human advice.

At Eva Wealth, we know not everyone is ready, or needs, full financial planning straight away. Our response to this has been to develop a digital platform, MyWealthVault, designed to provide an affordable, self-paced introduction to managing your money. But it doesn't stop there as we recognise the importance of access to an adviser when needed and so the platform allows you to chat and meet with an adviser for ad hoc sessions where required if you ever want a little more interaction or reassurance.

With technology moving so quickly, it won't be long before there's a whole spectrum of services available, making different levels of financial advice more accessible to more people than ever. The important thing is that you can choose the level of support that feels right for you at each stage of your journey.

Final Thoughts

Finding the right financial professional isn't just about technical expertise, it's about trust, respect, and feeling empowered. The right adviser should make you feel more in control, not less. If you walk away from a meeting feeling small or confused, that's your cue to keep looking.

Remember: you are allowed to ask questions, set boundaries, and walk away. This is your financial journey, and any professional you bring on board is there to serve as your partner, not your boss.

Chapter 18: Working with Financial Professionals

1. **Quick Knowledge Check**: I would consider working with a financial adviser when:
   - ☐ I have complex needs
   - ☐ Major life changes
   - ☐ Feeling overwhelmed
   - ☐ Never – I prefer DIY

2. **One Key Reflection:** My biggest concern about working with a financial adviser is:
   - ☐ Cost
   - ☐ Finding someone I trust
   - ☐ Losing control
   - ☐ Not having enough money

3. **Priority Action This Week:**
   - ☐ Research what types of financial professionals exist
   - ☐ Check what financial advice my employer provides
   - ☐ Write down questions I'd want to ask a potential adviser

Chapter 19:
Passing It On – Sharing Your Financial Wisdom

One of the most powerful legacies we can leave isn't money itself, but the knowledge of how to use it well. Teaching children and grandchildren about money equips them with skills and confidence that will serve them for a lifetime.

If we think about how we learned about money, often it was the hard way, through trial, error, and mistakes that could have been avoided if someone had guided us earlier. By gently passing on financial wisdom, we give the next generation the head start most of us never had.

And here's the good news: teaching children about money doesn't require you to be an expert. You don't need to know everything about pensions or investing. What matters most is making conversations about money normal, practical, and free from shame.

Start Early, Keep It Simple

Children form their attitudes about money surprisingly young – research shows basic money habits can be shaped by the age of seven. That doesn't mean we should start talking about stock markets in primary school, but it does mean early lessons stick.

Young children (5–10): Introduce simple ideas like saving, spending, and sharing. You might use three jars or labelled envelopes so they can physically divide their pocket money. Everyday experiences, like choosing whether to spend on sweets now or save for a bigger toy later, create natural learning moments.

Tweens and teens (1–18): As children grow, they can handle bigger concepts like budgeting, compound interest, or the difference between wants and needs. Let them help plan the weekly food shop with a budget. Show them how interest grows in a savings account. If appropriate, open a Junior ISA or savings account and review statements together.

Young adults (18+): By the time they're stepping into independence, practical knowledge becomes vital. Credit scores, managing overdrafts, student loans, or the importance of starting to invest early are key topics. Share your own experiences, including the mistakes. Sometimes the stories of what we'd do differently are the most powerful lessons of all.

Joy & Choice

This pot gives children immediate enjoyment and autonomy.

It teaches:

- Everyday decision-making
- Delayed vs. instant gratification
- Comparing value ('Is this worth my money?')

Security & Future You

This is their first taste of building a safety net.

It teaches:

- Planning
- Setting goals
- Watching money grow over time

Kindness & Community

This pot creates a lifelong connection between money and values.

It teaches:

- Purpose
- Generosity
- Understanding how resources help others

Everyday Teaching Moments

Teaching doesn't need to feel like "a lesson." In fact, the best learning often comes through ordinary life.

- **Shopping trips:** Talk through decisions about price comparisons, value for money, or why buying in bulk sometimes works and sometimes doesn't.
- **Holidays**: Involve them in saving towards a trip or managing a holiday budget.
- **Big purchases:** Explain how you plan and save for a car, a renovation, or even Christmas. Let them see that bigger goals require patience and planning.
- **Mistakes:** If you've overspent one month or missed out on a deal, share it honestly. Children learn resilience and problem-solving when they see that even adults make mistakes and recover.

These real-world moments are far more memorable than abstract talks.

Making It Engaging

Different ages typically learn best in different ways. Here are some approaches that can help to keep money learning engaging:

- **Games and challenges:** Younger children love setting saving goals with visual trackers (like colouring in a chart as their savings grow). Teens might enjoy challenges such as "plan a family meal for £10."
- **Stories and examples:** Share family stories – maybe how grandparents saved for their first home, or how you handled money as a student. These stories stick far longer than lectures.
- **Technology:** Budgeting and savings apps designed for children and teens can make the process interactive and fun.
- **Shared projects:** Encourage them to save for something they truly want. The pride of buying it themselves is a lesson that lasts.

Common Challenges (and How to Overcome Them)

Money conversations with children aren't always straightforward. Here are some hurdles you might encounter:

- **"I don't care about money":** Children, especially teenagers, may resist. Keep it relevant by linking money to things they value – freedom, choices, independence.
- **Impatience:** Saving for the future can feel abstract. Visual trackers, short-term rewards, and celebrating milestones help maintain motivation.
- **Peer pressure:** Children and teens face enormous pressure to "keep up." Encourage them to think critically about trends, and model mindful spending yourself.
- **Your own discomfort:** If you feel awkward talking about money, acknowledge it honestly. Tell your child, *"I didn't learn this when I was young, so I want us to figure it out together."* That honesty in itself is a powerful lesson.

The Long-Term Impact

Teaching children about money isn't just about pounds and pence. It's about building confidence, independence, and resilience. Children who grow up with positive money habits are:

- Less likely to get into unmanageable debt.
- More likely to save and invest early.
- Better prepared to navigate big life milestones, from university to buying a home.
- More confident negotiating pay and making informed financial choices.

And perhaps most importantly, they're more likely to pass on these habits to their own children. This is how we create generational change: by breaking cycles of financial struggle and replacing them with cycles of financial confidence.

Passing It On To Grandchildren

If you're a grandparent, you have a beautiful role to play. Conversations about money may be easier coming from you (one step removed from the daily parent-child dynamic).

Practical ways to get involved include:

- Setting up savings accounts or Junior ISAs as gifts.
- Involving grandchildren in conversations about family traditions like holiday spending or charitable giving.
- Sharing stories about how money was managed in your generation, both the struggles and the strategies.

Grandparents are often in a privileged position; grandchildren often listen closely to grandparents in ways they might not with parents. Your perspective carries weight.

A Gentle Challenge

Think about one simple money habit you wish you'd learned earlier. Now imagine how different your financial journey might have been if you'd known it at age 10 or 15.

That's the power you hold in your hands right now, to give that lesson to your children or grandchildren.

So ask yourself: *what one money conversation can I start this week?*

Because your greatest financial legacy may not be the money you leave behind, but the wisdom and confidence you pass on while you're here.

Chapter 19: Teaching Others – Sharing Financial Wisdom

1. **Quick Knowledge Check:** I feel comfortable discussing money with:
   - ☐ Anyone
   - ☐ Close family
   - ☐ Partner only
   - ☐ No one really

2. **One Key Reflection:** The most important money lesson I'd want to pass on is:

3. **Priority Action This Week:**
   - ☐ Have one age-appropriate money conversation with a child in my life
   - ☐ Share one financial insight with a friend who might benefit
   - ☐ Practice explaining one money concept in simple terms

Chapter 20:
Your Financial Freedom Journey

Ask ten women what financial freedom means, and you'll hear ten very different answers. For some, it's being able to walk away from a job that drains them, without worrying about the next pay check. For others, it's the relief of knowing that if life throws a curveball – an illness, a redundancy, a boiler that finally gives up; they can handle it. And for others still, it's about abundance: building enough wealth that choices feel limitless, not restricted.

Your definition of financial freedom is personal. It doesn't need to look like anyone else's, and it may well change as you move through different stages of life. What felt like freedom in your twenties (the ability to travel or live without debt) might feel very different in your fifties (funding your children's education, scaling back work, or supporting causes close to your heart). Here are some common threads that women describe when they reach for the words "financial freedom":

- The ability to choose how to spend your time, without money dictating every decision
- Feeling calm and secure about the future rather than fearful or uncertain
- Having the confidence to weather emergencies without panic
- Knowing you can support the people and causes that matter most to you

Above all, financial freedom means flipping the script: money becomes a tool to create the life you want, rather than a source of constant stress.

HEDONIC ADAPTATION
We quickly adapt to new levels of income or lifestyle, which is why financial freedom isn't just about "more." True freedom comes from aligning money with values and purpose, not endlessly chasing the next upgrade. Recognising this pattern helps you build lasting contentment.

The Psychology of Financial Freedom

It's easy to assume financial freedom is about numbers, but mindset plays just as big a role.

Many of us carry quiet money beliefs we've picked up from family, society, or past experiences. They sound like:

- "I'm just not good with money."
- "Wealthy people are greedy."
- "I don't deserve financial success."

Left unchecked, these beliefs act like invisible barriers, quietly holding us back. But the good news is they are just stories, and stories can be rewritten.

Try reframing:

- "I'm learning to manage my money with confidence."
- "Wealth gives me choices and the ability to make an impact."
- "I am worthy of security and freedom."

Building a wealth mindset isn't about ignoring risk or pretending everything will always go smoothly. It's about approaching money from a place of possibility instead of fear.

QUICK CHECK-IN: Write down one limiting belief you've carried about money. Now rewrite it into an empowering statement you want to believe. Keep it somewhere visible (a post-it on your mirror, or the front of your journal).

The Stages of Financial Freedom

Think of financial freedom as a staircase. Each stage builds on the one before, and each brings its own sense of achievement:

1. **Financial Stability:** You've built an emergency fund, tackled high-interest debt, and stopped living pay check-to-pay check. Life feels less frantic. If your washing machine breaks, it's inconvenient, not a crisis.

2. **Financial Security:** You've added breathing room: savings are growing, investments are building, debt is manageable. You may still rely on work for income, but you're no longer living with the fear of "what if?" every month.

3. **Financial Independence:** Your investments could theoretically cover your core expenses. You may still work, but the crucial shift is this: you're working because you want to, not because you have to.

4. **Financial Freedom:** Your money more than covers your lifestyle. You have genuine choice about how to spend your time. Work becomes optional. Supporting loved ones or backing causes you care about is within reach.

FINANCIAL FREEDOM STAIRCASE

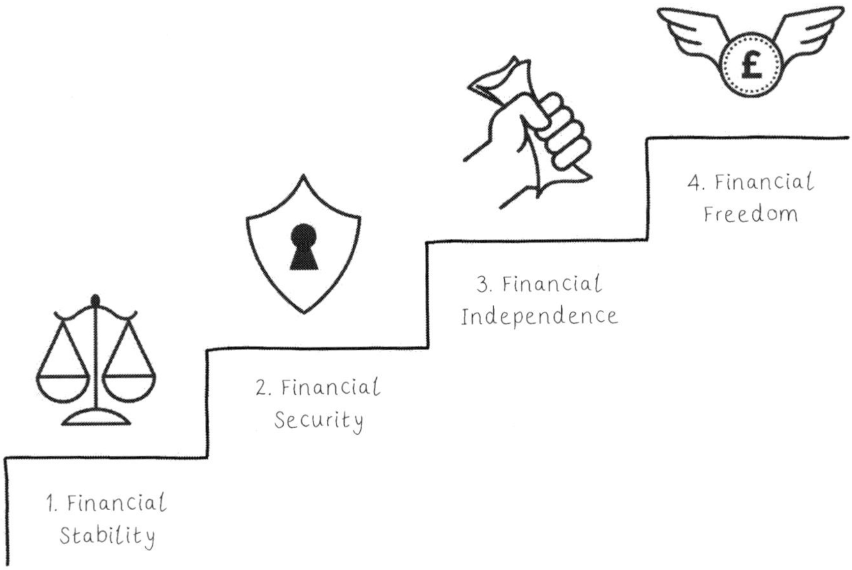

QUICK CHECK-IN: Identify Your Stage. Which stage feels most like where you are now? Which stage feels like the next natural milestone for you? Write down one practical step that could move you closer.

Accelerating Progress

While wealth-building takes time, there are ways to move faster:

- **Increase Your Income:** Upskill, negotiate that pay rise, or create an additional stream (consulting, side hustle, investing in your expertise). Every pound earned and invested compounds over time.
- **Optimise Spending:** Cut the "leaks" that don't bring joy (unused subscriptions, inflated bills). Protect the spending that does matter.

- **Maximise Investments:** Focus on what you can control; fees, diversification, tax-efficiency. Over decades, these small improvements can be game-changing.
- **Use Tax-Advantaged Accounts:** Maximise pensions and ISAs. The tax relief and growth potential make these some of the most powerful tools available.

Staying Motivated Along the Way

Freedom doesn't happen overnight, so staying motivated is key.

- **Celebrate milestones:** the first £1,000 in savings, paying off a credit card, reaching £10,000 invested. Each one matters.
- **Visualise your why:** create a vision board, write a letter to your future self, or use journaling to connect with the feelings of freedom.
- **Find community:** join an investment club, women's money circle, HerWealthVault, or simply share your goals with a trusted friend. Walking this path with others makes it less lonely.
- **Track your progress:** reviewing your net worth and financial wins monthly can help you see how small steps build into something powerful.

Common Obstacles and How to Overcome Them

- **Market Volatility:** Markets will always rise and fall. The key is perspective. A dip is a season, not the end of the story.
- **Lifestyle Inflation:** More income often tempts more spending. Build in automatic increases to savings when your pay rises.
- **Unexpected Big Costs:** Robust emergency funds and the right insurance act as shock absorbers.
- **Changing Goals:** It's okay to pivot. Your financial plan should evolve with you, not tie you to past versions of yourself.

QUICK CHECK-IN: Which obstacle feels most likely to derail you? Write down one practical system that could help protect against it.

Beyond Yourself: The Ripple Effect

One of the most powerful parts of this journey is what it unlocks beyond your own life.

When you achieve financial freedom, you don't just benefit yourself. You inspire your children, encourage your peers, and contribute to closing the gender wealth gap. You show others what's possible and your ripple effect is bigger than you may ever realise.

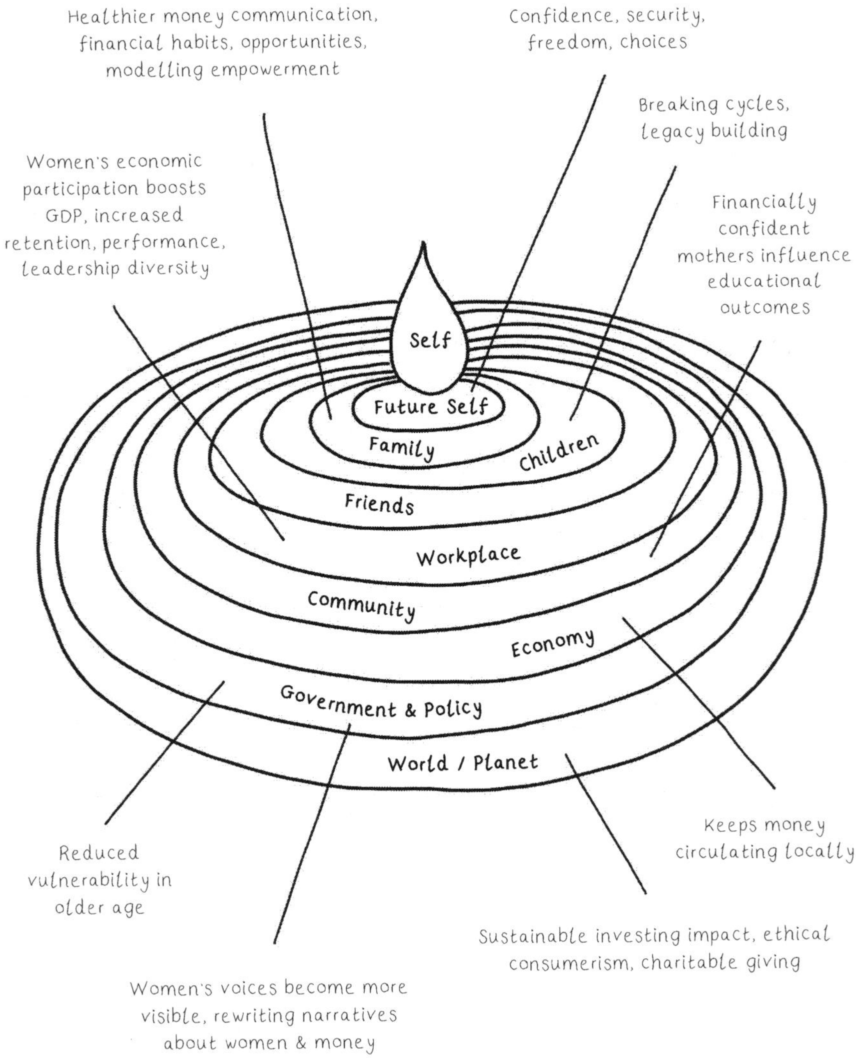

Enjoying the Journey

A vital reminder: don't delay joy until "someday." Financial freedom is about designing a life you love now as well as in the future.

Build fun into your plan. Budget for travel, flowers on the table, or that experience you've longed for. Money is there to serve you, not punish you. Balance discipline with delight.

Your Archetype's Path to Financial Freedom

As we conclude this journey together, remember that financial freedom looks different for each money story archetype, and that's perfectly okay.

Status Seekers: Your freedom comes from building wealth that creates genuine security and options, not just the appearance of success. True status is having the choice to live life on your own terms. Your drive for achievement, when channelled into real wealth building, becomes unstoppable.

Guardians: Your freedom is the deep security that comes from knowing you're prepared for whatever life brings. Your careful planning creates unshakeable confidence. Your natural saving ability, when combined with strategic growth, builds lasting wealth.

Free Spirits: Your freedom is having enough resources to say yes to the experiences and values that matter most to you, without financial stress clouding your joy. Your generous spirit, supported by smart systems, creates both financial security and life satisfaction.

Avoiders: Your freedom is the peace that comes from having systems that work without constant attention, allowing you to focus on what you do best. Your desire for simplicity, when channelled into automated wealth building, creates effortless prosperity.

The Evolution of Your Money Story

Remember, you are not locked into your archetype forever. As you grow and develop financial confidence, you might find yourself incorporating positive traits from other archetypes. A Guardian might develop some Free Spirit joy in spending, or an Avoider might gain some Status Seeker ambition for wealth building. This is growth, not inconsistency.

Your money story is a living, evolving narrative. Every financial decision you make is a sentence in that story. Make it a story worth telling.

Financial empowerment isn't about never making mistakes. It's about learning, adjusting, and moving forward with resilience. Every pound saved, every step toward investing, every brave money conversation – they all add up.

Your path is yours alone. Don't let comparison steal your joy. Instead, celebrate progress and trust the process.

And remember: when one woman grows in financial confidence, the world around her shifts too. You're not just creating security for yourself – you're modelling what's possible for others.

Chapter 20 Workbook Exercises: Your Financial Freedom Journey

1. Quick Knowledge Check: Financial freedom to me means:

- ☐ Never worrying about money
- ☐ Retiring early
- ☐ Having choices
- ☐ Helping others

2. Rate your current progress toward financial freedom (1–10):

3. One Key Reflection: The biggest change I need to make to achieve financial freedom is:

4. Priority Action This Week:

- ☐ Define what financial freedom looks like for me specifically
- ☐ Calculate my "freedom number"
- ☐ Identify the one habit that would have the biggest impact on my journey

Your Next Steps

You've journeyed through this book, page by page, story by story. And if you've made it this far, here's what I know: you are committed. That commitment matters more than any technical concept or financial strategy.

As you close this book, choose one small action to take this week. It could be:

- Updating your budget
- Opening your first investment account
- Setting up a monthly transfer to savings
- Having a "money date" with your partner
- Reviewing your pension or insurance cover
- Sharing something you've learned with a friend
- The action itself matters less than the fact you begin. Small, imperfect steps compound into extraordinary change.

What Comes Next: Your Ongoing Journey

There will be bumps. Markets will wobble, life will surprise you, and you'll sometimes doubt yourself. That's normal. What matters is that you keep going.

You already have everything you need: intelligence, determination, and now, knowledge. There will be more to learn along the way and also time to revisit previous learnings – because it is often only when we can truly apply the knowledge we have gained that it takes on a deeper level of meaning and understanding.

So, take that next step with courage. Your money, your future, your freedom – they're already within your grasp.

At Eva Wealth we recognise that the question that is often asked is "what happens next?". So we have created MyWealthVault to help you with your onward journey. MyWealthVault is the next evolution in women's financial empowerment. It has been designed to bridge the advice gap and transform how women engage with their money.

Built from the belief that financial wellbeing is about far more than numbers, MyWealthVault combines expert financial insight with emotional intelligence and behavioural design. It's a digital ecosystem that helps women at every stage of life understand, organise, and grow their wealth with clarity, confidence, and purpose.

Inside the platform, you can access guided learning pathways, personalised tools, and actionable insights, all designed to support real progress, not overwhelm. From mastering cash flow to planning for retirement, from understanding investments to aligning money with personal values, MyWealthVault helps you to take consistent, confident steps forward.

But this isn't just about better money management. It's about reclaiming power. MyWealthVault represents a shift in how women experience financial planning. We are building a community that is collaborative, eager and rooted in self-awareness. It's where practical strategy meets personal growth – a place to rewrite your money story, one empowered decision at a time.

Because financial freedom isn't just about having wealth. It's about feeling safe, supported, and in control of your future. MyWealthVault is here to make that possible – for every woman, at every stage of her journey.

Welcome to your financial future. It's going to be extraordinary.

Acknowledgements

To every woman who has trusted me to walk alongside her through financial change, thank you. Your courage, honesty, and determination inspired *Smart Money, Strong Women* and continue to guide my work every day. This book exists because of the questions you've asked, the vulnerabilities you've shared, and the transformations you've achieved.

To the many friends, colleagues, and family members who have offered encouragement, ideas, and perspective along the way, your belief in this project has mattered more than you know. You've each played an important role, not only in bringing this manuscript together, but in reminding me to keep pushing forward when the path felt uncertain. I can't list you all here, but you know who you are. A special thank you to Suze, Sarah, and Emily for your unwavering support.

Thank you to Jen and Marianna for reading through my first draft and offering such thoughtful, constructive feedback. Marianna, your gorgeous illustrations brought warmth and personality to these pages in ways words alone never could.

And to my beautiful family, who have graciously allowed me to pursue this work, often at the expense of time together. Your patience, love, and faith have meant everything. Thank you for believing in this book, and in me, even when it meant more late nights, distracted conversations, and "just five more minutes" at my laptop. This journey is only just beginning, and I'm grateful to be taking you on it with me.

Technical Appendices for Smart Money, Strong Women

IMPORTANT DISCLAIMER: The information in these appendices is for educational purposes only and should not be considered personal financial advice. Investment values can go down as well as up, and you may get back less than you invest. Past performance is not a guide to future performance. Tax rules can change and their benefits depend on your individual circumstances. You should always seek professional financial advice before making investment decisions.

Appendix A: Investment Fundamentals – Educational Framework

IMPORTANT DISCLAIMER: This appendix provides general educational information about investment concepts commonly discussed in the UK market. It is not financial advice and should not be treated as a personal recommendation. Investment decisions should always be based on your complete financial situation, goals, and risk tolerance. Consider speaking with a qualified, regulated financial adviser before making investment decisions.

A1: Platform Research Framework

When researching investment platforms, you'll typically encounter three broad approaches. Understanding which aligns with your preferences can help narrow your research:

Step 1: Determine Your Investment Approach

- **DIY Investor approach:** You research and select individual funds or shares yourself
- **Guided Investor approach:** You want help with portfolio construction and fund selection
- **Hands-off Investor approach:** You prefer professional management or algorithm-based (robo) advice

Step 2: Platform Comparison Criteria

Different platform types typically have different cost structures and features:

Feature	DIY Platforms	Guided Platforms	Robo-Advisors
Typical Annual Platform Fee	0.15–0.45%	0.35–0.75%	0.25–0.85%
Dealing Charges	£1.50–£11.95 per trade	Often included	Usually included
Fund Selection	Typically 1000+ options	Curated selection	Algorithm selected
Research Tools	Usually comprehensive	Basic to intermediate	Often limited
Human Support	Generally limited	Usually available	Typically limited

Note: Fees and features vary significantly between providers. These ranges are for illustration only.

Platform Features to Research

When researching DIY platforms, commonly available features include:

- Annual charges typically ranging from 0.15–0.45%
- Wide fund selection (often 1000+ options)
- Research and screening tools
- Various dealing charge structures

When researching guided platforms, look for information about:

- Risk-based portfolio construction approaches
- Professional fund selection services
- Automatic rebalancing services
- Educational resources and support availability

When researching robo-advisory services, common features include:

- Algorithm-based portfolio construction
- Varying minimum investment requirements
- Automatic rebalancing
- Risk assessment questionnaires
- Key Research Considerations

Cost analysis:

- Compare total annual costs for your intended investment amount
- Consider whether fixed-fee or percentage-based charging works better for your situation
- Check for hidden fees (exit charges, transfer fees, inactivity fees)

Functionality needs:

- If interested in individual shares: Check for equity research tools
- If preferring simplicity: Look for curated fund selections and straightforward interfaces
- Regular investing: Assess ease of setting up automated contributions

Questions to ask when researching platforms:

- What are the total annual costs for my intended investment amount?
- What research and educational tools are provided?
- How easy is it to set up regular investing?
- What customer service and goes wrong (FSCS protection)?

Important note: The cheapest platform isn't always the best choice if it doesn't meet your specific needs. Consider functionality, support, and ease of use alongside cost.

A2: Investment Fund Education Framework

Step 1: Understanding Asset Allocation Concepts

Asset allocation refers to how investments are divided between different asset types (equities, bonds, cash, property, etc.). Many factors influence appropriate asset allocation, and there's no one-size-fits-all answer.

Common Age-Based Asset Allocation Examples:

Financial commentary often references age-based equity allocations as rough starting points for research. **These are illustrative examples only and may not be appropriate for your circumstances:**

- **20s–30s:** Commentators often discuss higher equity allocations (e.g., 80–90%) for those with very long time horizons
- **40s:** Balanced approaches with some defensive assets (e.g., 70–80% equities) are commonly discussed
- **50s:** Discussions often include beginning to reduce equity exposure (e.g., 60–70% equities)
- **60s+:** Focus typically shifts more toward capital preservation (e.g., 50–60% equities)

Critical factors that influence asset allocation (often more important than age alone):

- **Risk capacity:** How much potential loss can you financially absorb without derailing your goals?
- **Time horizon:** When will you need to access this money?
- **Risk tolerance:** How comfortable are you with investment volatility and potential losses?
- **Other income sources:** Do you have guaranteed pension income, rental income, or other assets?
- **Financial goals:** Are you focused on growth, income generation, or capital preservation?
- **Existing assets:** What other investments and resources do you have?
- **Life circumstances:** Dependents, job security, health, and many other personal factors

These factors interact in complex ways. What's appropriate for one 45-year-old may be completely inappropriate for another 45-year-old with different circumstances.

Step 2: Geographic Diversification Concepts

Investment diversification across geographies is a common risk management approach. Commentary on geographic diversification often discusses ranges such as:

- UK: 20–40% (home bias consideration without overconcentration)
- Developed International Markets: 40–60%
- Emerging Markets: 5–15%
- Bonds: Mix of UK government and corporate

These percentages are examples from financial commentary, not recommendations. Appropriate geographic diversification depends on numerous factors including your circumstances, existing assets, currency considerations, and investment goals.

Step 3: Active vs Passive Fund Considerations

Passive (Index) Funds – Common Characteristics:

- Typically lower costs than active funds
- Track a market index rather than trying to beat it
- Require less active decision-making
- Often considered appropriate for long-term investing

When passive funds are commonly discussed as potentially suitable:

- Investors seeking low-cost exposure
- Those who believe markets are generally efficient
- Preference for simplicity
- Long-term investment horizons (often cited as 10+ years)

Active Funds – Common Characteristics:

- Professional fund managers make investment decisions
- Typically higher fees than passive funds
- Attempt to outperform market indices
- May focus on specific themes or strategies

When active funds are commonly discussed as potentially suitable:

- Willingness to pay higher fees for potential (not guaranteed) outperformance
- Interest in specific themes (e.g., ESG, specific sectors, geographic regions)

- Desire for professional management during volatile periods
- Certain market segments where active management may add value (e.g., smaller companies, emerging markets)

Important considerations: Past performance doesn't guarantee future results. Many active funds fail to outperform their benchmarks over long periods, especially after fees.

Step 4: Fund Type Categories

Investment literature often discusses portfolio construction using "core" and "satellite" approaches:

"Core Holdings" Concept (often discussed as 70–80% of portfolio):
Core holdings typically refer to broad, diversified funds that form the foundation of a portfolio:

- **Global Equity Funds:** Provide exposure across multiple countries and sectors
- **UK Equity Funds:** Exposure to UK companies across various sizes
- **Bond Funds:** Government bonds (typically lower risk) and corporate bonds (typically higher yield but more risk)

"Satellite Holdings" Concept (often discussed as 20–30% of portfolio):
Satellite holdings typically refer to more specialised or targeted investments:

- **Emerging Market Funds:** Potential for higher growth but typically higher volatility
- **ESG/Sustainable Funds:** Investment approaches aligned with environmental, social, and governance criteria
- **Property Funds:** Real estate exposure through REITs and property companies
- **Sector-specific funds:** Technology, healthcare, financial services, etc.

Research Considerations When Evaluating Funds:

- **Ongoing Charges Figure (OCF):** Total annual cost of holding the fund
- **Track record:** Performance over multiple market cycles (remembering past performance doesn't guarantee future results)
- **Fund size and liquidity:** Ability to buy and sell without significant impact
- **Investment approach:** Active vs passive, investment style
- **Manager tenure:** For actively managed funds, how long has the current manager been in place?

Illustrative Asset Allocation Example

Financial publications sometimes show example portfolios for educational purposes. Here's one example that might be discussed for a 35-year-old with a long time horizon and moderate-to-high risk tolerance:

- 40% Global Developed Market Equities
- 20% UK Equities
- 10% Emerging Market Equities
- 15% ESG/Sustainable Equity Funds
- 10% Government/Corporate Bonds
- 5% Property/REITs

CRITICAL DISCLAIMER: This is a hypothetical example for educational purposes only and should not be considered suitable for any specific individual. Appropriate asset allocation depends on your complete financial situation, goals, risk capacity, risk tolerance, time horizon, and numerous other personal factors. Do not implement any allocation without professional advice tailored to your circumstances.

Rebalancing Considerations

Rebalancing refers to adjusting your portfolio back to target allocations when market movements cause drift. Common approaches discussed in investment literature include:

- Reviewing allocations quarterly or annually
- Considering rebalancing when allocations drift 5%+ from targets
- Using new contributions to buy underweight assets rather than selling
- Considering tax implications before selling in taxable accounts

Whether and how to rebalance depends on your specific situation, tax position, and investment strategy.

A3: Investment Account Optimisation

This section provides educational information about common UK tax-advantaged accounts. Tax rules are complex and change frequently. Always verify current rules and seek professional advice about your specific tax situation.

Individual Savings Account (ISA) – Key Features

Current rules (2024/25 tax year):

- Annual subscription limit: £20,000
- Investment growth and withdrawals are free from income tax and capital gains tax

- Can be split between Cash ISA and Stocks & Shares ISA (within overall £20,000 limit)
- Flexible ISAs allow withdrawals and replacements within the same tax year

Common ISA strategy considerations discussed in financial planning:

- Using the annual allowance if financially feasible
- Prioritising higher-growth assets in the ISA wrapper (since tax-free growth has more impact)
- Considering asset location across different account types based on tax efficiency

Pension vs ISA – Key Differences

These are two very different vehicles with different features:

Feature	Pension	ISA
Tax relief on contributions	Yes (20–45% depending on rate)	No
Tax on growth	Tax-free	Tax-free
Access	Age 55+ (rising to 57 in 2028)	Any time
Tax on withdrawal	25% tax-free, rest taxed as income	Tax-free
Inheritance tax	Usually outside estate	Part of estate
Annual limit	£60,000 (or 100% of earnings if less)	£20,000

Factors to consider when deciding between pension and ISA contributions:

- Your marginal tax rate now vs expected retirement tax rate
- When you'll need access to the money
- Your other pension provision
- Inheritance planning considerations
- Overall financial circumstances and goals

Common considerations discussed for different taxpayers:

- **Basic rate taxpayers:** Get 20% tax relief on pension contributions; might value ISA flexibility for earlier access
- **Higher rate taxpayers:** Get 40% tax relief on pension contributions; significant immediate benefit but money locked until pension access age
- **Additional rate taxpayers:** Get 45% tax relief; even stronger case for pensions from pure tax perspective

These are general observations, not recommendations. The right answer depends on your complete situation.

General Investment Account (GIA) Considerations
A GIA is a standard taxable investment account, typically used only after maximising tax-advantaged accounts (ISAs and pensions).

Key tax considerations for GIAs:

- Dividends are subject to dividend tax (after £500 dividend allowance in 2024/25)
- Capital gains are subject to CGT (after £3,000 annual exempt amount in 2024/25)
- Can utilise annual CGT allowance by realising gains strategically
- Can "harvest" losses to offset gains

GIA strategies commonly discussed:

- Using GIAs only after maximising ISA and pension allowances
- Selling and repurchasing investments (outside ISAs) to utilise annual CGT allowance
- Timing capital gains across tax years
- Loss harvesting to offset gains

Important: Tax rules are complex and change frequently. Consider professional tax advice for your specific situation.

FINAL REMINDER: This appendix provides educational information about investment concepts and UK market structures. Nothing in this appendix constitutes financial advice or personal recommendations. Investment decisions should be based on professional advice tailored to your complete financial circumstances, goals, and risk tolerance.

Appendix B: Pension Planning – Educational Framework

CRITICAL PENSION DISCLAIMER: Pension planning is one of the most complex areas of personal finance, involving intricate tax rules, changing regulations, and highly individual circumstances. The information in this appendix is for educational purposes only and provides a general overview of pension concepts commonly discussed in the UK market.

This is not pension advice. Pension decisions can have irreversible consequences and should always be based on professional advice specific to your circumstances. This is particularly critical for:

- Pension transfers, especially from defined benefit (final salary) schemes
- Drawdown vs annuity decisions
- Divorce-related pension considerations
- Inheritance planning involving pensions

Pension rules change frequently. Verify current rules before making any decisions, and always consult a qualified, FCA-regulated pension adviser.

B1: Understanding Pension Contribution Limits

Pension contribution limits in the UK involve several rules that interact in complex ways. This section provides an overview of key concepts.

Annual Allowance (2024/25: £60,000)

The annual allowance is the maximum amount that can be contributed to pensions in a tax year while still receiving tax relief. Key points:

- Applies to total contributions from all sources (personal, employer, third party)
- Includes both your contributions and employer contributions
- Reduces (tapers) for high earners with adjusted income over £260,000
- Different rules may apply if you have already accessed pension benefits ("money purchase annual allowance")

Carry Forward Rules – Overview

UK pension rules allow unused annual allowance from the previous three tax years to be carried forward. Key features:

- Must have been a member of a UK registered pension scheme in the years you're carrying forward from
- Current year's allowance must be used first before carry forward
- Unused allowance from earliest year is used first
- Complex interactions with tapered allowance for high earners

Illustrative Carry Forward Example

This example illustrates how carry forward might work in a specific scenario. **This is not advice and your situation will differ.**

Hypothetical scenario: Sarah earns £50,000 annually and has historically contributed £5,000 per year to her pension for the past three years:

- Current year (2024/25) allowance: £60,000
- Year 1 (2021/22) unused: £55,000
- Year 2 (2022/23) unused: £55,000
- Year 3 (2023/24) unused: £55,000
- Theoretical total available (current year + carry forward): £225,000

If Sarah received a £100,000 bonus and wanted to make a large pension contribution, she would theoretically have sufficient unused allowance to contribute a significant portion. At a 40% tax rate, the tax relief on a £100,000 contribution would be £40,000.

Important caveats:

- This example assumes Sarah remains a member of a pension scheme throughout
- Doesn't account for potential tapered allowance issues
- Tax relief depends on earnings and tax position
- Doesn't consider whether such a large contribution is appropriate for her circumstances
- Carry forward calculations can be complex; professional advice is essential for large contributions.

B2: Pension Contributions and Employment Status

How you contribute to a pension and receive tax relief differs based on employment status. This section outlines common scenarios.

Employed Individuals – Salary Sacrifice Arrangements

Some employers offer "salary sacrifice" (also called "salary exchange") pension arrangements. Understanding how these work:

What is salary sacrifice?

- You agree to reduce your contractual salary
- Your employer contributes the "sacrificed" amount to your pension
- Both you and your employer may save National Insurance contributions
- You still receive full tax relief on the pension contribution

Potential benefits commonly discussed:

- Saves employee National Insurance (currently 8% on earnings £12,570–£50,270, 2% above)
- Saves employer National Insurance (13.8% on most earnings)
- Some employers share their NI saving by contributing more to your pension
- May affect certain means-tested benefits or statutory payments

Potential considerations:

- Reduces your "official" salary which might affect mortgage applications
- May impact life insurance or income protection based on salary multiples
- Could affect statutory maternity/paternity pay calculations
- Must maintain minimum wage after sacrifice

Illustrative Salary Sacrifice Calculation:

Hypothetical scenario: Someone earning £60,000 wants to contribute £10,000 to their pension. This example compares two methods:

Method 1: Via Salary Sacrifice

- Agreed reduced salary: £50,000
- Employer contributes £10,000 to pension
- Income tax saving: £4,000 (40% on £10,000)

- National Insurance saving: £200 (2% on £10,000 for amounts over £50,270)
- Total personal saving: £4,200
- Net cost to individual: £5,800

Method 2: Via Personal Contribution

- Salary remains £60,000
- Individual contributes from net (after-tax) pay
- Takes home approximately £6,000 less
- Claims £4,000 tax relief via pension provider and/or tax return
- Net cost to individual: £6,000

Critical disclaimers for this example:

- Assumes specific tax code and no other deductions
- NI rates and thresholds change regularly
- Doesn't account for employer NI savings potentially being shared
- Individual circumstances vary significantly
- This illustration should not be used for decision-making without professional advice

Self-Employed – Personal Pension Contributions

Self-employed individuals contribute to personal pensions differently than employees:

Contribution limits:

- Lower of £60,000 or 100% of relevant UK earnings (whichever is less)
- "Relevant UK earnings" typically means self-employment income, not turnover
- Carry forward rules apply (same as for employed individuals)
- Can base contributions on either current or previous tax year's earnings

Tax relief mechanism:

- Contributions are made "net" of basic rate tax relief
- Pension provider claims 20% basic rate relief from HMRC and adds to pension
- Higher and additional rate taxpayers claim extra relief via Self Assessment tax return
- Relief given at your marginal rate up to contribution limits

Illustrative Self-Employed Example

Hypothetical scenario: Self-employed person with £80,000 taxable profit wants to make a £20,000 gross pension contribution:

How it works:

- They pay: £16,000 to pension provider
- Pension provider claims from HMRC: £4,000 (basic rate relief)
- Total in pension pot: £20,000
- They claim via tax return: Additional £4,000 (higher rate relief, 40%–20% = 20% on £20,000)
- Effective cost after all relief: £12,000 for £20,000 gross contribution

Important considerations:

- Assumes 40% taxpayer throughout
- Must have sufficient earnings to support contribution
- Tax relief claimed via Self Assessment can be complex
- Timing of relief receipt varies (pension provider relief is immediate, additional relief comes via tax return)
- This is a simplified illustration; actual tax position may be more complex

B3: Pension Investment Considerations

Pension investments are typically held for very long periods. This section discusses common approaches to pension investment strategy.

Asset Allocation Concepts Over Time

Financial commentary often discusses how pension asset allocation might evolve as people age. **These are general concepts, not recommendations:**

Longer Time Horizons (e.g., 20s–30s) – Common Discussion Points:

- Often discussed: Higher allocation to growth assets (equities) due to long time to recover from volatility
- Many commentators suggest equity-heavy portfolios for younger investors
- Low-cost index funds are frequently recommended for long-term pension investing
- The principle "time in market" is often valued over "timing the market"

Medium Time Horizons (e.g., 40s–50s) – Common Discussion Points:

- Balanced approach often discussed: maintaining significant growth assets while beginning diversification
- Gradual introduction of defensive assets (bonds) commonly mentioned
- Target-date funds (which automatically adjust allocation) are often discussed for this life stage
- Regular review becomes more important as retirement approaches

Approaching Retirement (e.g., 55+) – Common Discussion Points:

- Gradual reduction in equity exposure is often discussed
- Increased focus on capital preservation
- Planning how to access pension becomes critical
- Coordination with other income sources (State Pension, other pensions, savings)

Critical limitations of age-based guidance:

- Everyone's risk capacity and tolerance differ
- Pension pot size matters enormously
- Other assets and income sources are highly relevant
- Health, dependents, and personal circumstances vary
- Investment markets and returns are unpredictable

Do not use age-based generalisations as the basis for investment decisions. Professional advice tailored to your complete situation is essential.

Pension Access Decisions – Key Concepts

When approaching pension access age (currently 55, rising to 57 in 2028), individuals typically face decisions about how to access their pension. Two main approaches are commonly discussed:

Pension Drawdown – Key Features:

- Keep pension invested and withdraw as needed
- Maintains potential for investment growth
- Also maintains investment risk (pot can go down)
- 25% typically available tax-free; remainder taxed as income when withdrawn
- Can pass remaining pension to beneficiaries (tax treatment depends on age at death)
- Requires ongoing investment decisions or advice
- No guaranteed income

Annuity – Key Features:

- Exchange pension pot for guaranteed income for life
- No investment risk once purchased
- Income amount fixed at purchase (unless inflation-linked annuity purchased)
- No remaining pot to pass to beneficiaries (except with certain annuity types)
- Decision is typically irreversible
- Rates vary based on health, age, and market conditions

FACTORS OFTEN CONSIDERED WHEN COMPARING THESE OPTIONS:

Drawdown might be discussed as potentially suitable when:

- You want to maintain investment control and potential growth
- You have other sources of guaranteed income (State Pension, DB pension, etc.)
- You're comfortable with investment risk and volatility
- Estate planning and passing on assets is important to you
- You want flexibility in withdrawal amounts

Annuity might be discussed as potentially suitable when:

- You prioritise certainty and guaranteed income
- You're risk-averse or don't want investment decisions
- You have limited other sources of secure income
- You have health conditions (may qualify for "enhanced" annuity rates with higher income)
- You value simplicity over flexibility

Critical considerations:

- This is one of the most important financial decisions you'll make
- The decision is often irreversible (especially annuity purchase)
- Tax implications are complex and highly individual
- You can combine approaches (annuity for some, drawdown for rest)
- Rates and rules change over time
- Professional advice is essential for this decision

Pension Withdrawal Rates – Academic Research

Academic research on sustainable withdrawal rates from retirement portfolios is often discussed in pension planning. Key concepts:

The "4% rule" and variations:

- Historical research suggested 4% annual withdrawal rate might be sustainable over 30-year retirement
- More recent research often suggests 3.5% may be more appropriate given current market conditions
- These are starting points for discussion, not guarantees
- Actual sustainable rate depends on: investment mix, market conditions, lifespan, spending flexibility, other income sources

Important limitations:

- Based on historical data which may not predict future results
- Assumes specific asset allocation (typically 50–75% equities)
- Doesn't account for flexible spending or income sources
- UK research may differ from US-based studies
- Individual circumstances vary enormously

Withdrawal planning should consider:

- Natural income from investments (dividends, interest)
- Capital withdrawals and impact on future sustainability
- Tax efficiency of withdrawals
- Coordination with State Pension and other income
- Flexibility to adjust spending based on circumstances

Professional financial planning is essential for drawdown strategies.

B4: Pensions and Major Life Events

Pensions are affected by many life events. This section provides educational overview of common scenarios.

Career Breaks and Pension Building

Taking time away from paid employment affects pension contributions:

Common considerations during career breaks:

- Employer contributions stop (if you leave employment)
- Personal contributions can continue to personal pensions (if you have relevant earnings)
- No relevant UK earnings = maximum £2,880 net contribution annually (£3,600 with tax relief)
- State Pension credits may be available for certain caring responsibilities

Return to work considerations:

- Employer matching contributions are valuable if available
- May have increased unused annual allowance from years with lower contributions (carry forward)
- Rebuilding pension contributions may compete with other financial priorities

Spousal pension arrangements:

- One spouse can contribute up to £2,880 net (£3,600 gross with relief) to the other's pension even with no earnings
- Useful for non-working spouses to maintain pension building
- Subject to annual allowance rules

Divorce and Pensions

Pensions are often one of the largest assets in divorce and are treated as matrimonial assets in UK law.

KEY CONCEPTS IN PENSION SHARING ON DIVORCE:

Pension Sharing Order:

- Court can order percentage of one person's pension to be transferred to the other
- Creates clean break – each party has their own pension
- Percentage is of the "Cash Equivalent Transfer Value" (CETV)
- Requires specialist pension on divorce advice (PODE)

Pension Offsetting:

- Pension value offset against other assets (e.g., one keeps pension, other keeps house)
- No transfer of actual pension
- Requires accurate valuation
- May have different tax treatments than actual values suggest

Pension Attachment Order:

- Less common
- One party receives income when other's pension is accessed
- Ongoing connection between parties

Critical considerations:

- Pension valuation in divorce is complex
- CETV may not reflect true value

- Defined benefit pensions require specialist valuation
- Tax implications differ for each approach
- Specialist divorce financial advice is essential
- This area is highly complex and this overview is not sufficient for decision-making

Inheritance and Pensions

Pensions have special inheritance tax treatment in the UK, making them potentially useful for estate planning:

KEY RULES (SUBJECT TO CHANGE):

Death before age 75:

- Pension pot typically passes tax-free to beneficiaries
- Beneficiaries can take as lump sum or income (both tax-free)
- Pension usually sits outside estate for inheritance tax purposes

Death after age 75:

- Pension pot still typically outside estate for IHT
- Beneficiaries pay income tax on withdrawals at their marginal rate
- Can still be passed on (unlike annuities with no death benefits)

Planning considerations often discussed:

- May be tax-efficient to spend other assets first and preserve pension
- Nomination of beneficiaries is important (not automatic to spouse)
- Rules interact with lifetime allowance history (for those with protections)
- Trust arrangements may be appropriate in some circumstances

Important limitations:

- Rules are complex and change frequently
- Interaction with other estate planning is crucial
- Not all pension schemes offer full death benefit flexibility
- May be challenged as inheritance tax avoidance if pension left untouched purely for this reason

Estate planning involving pensions requires professional advice from specialists in both pensions and inheritance tax.

Final Critical Reminders

1. **Pension rules are extraordinarily complex** and this appendix provides only a high-level educational overview.

2. **Pension decisions are often irreversible** – particularly transfers from defined benefit schemes and annuity purchases.

3. **Your circumstances are unique** – age, health, family situation, other assets, tax position, and goals all matter.

4. **Rules change frequently** – verify current rules before any decisions.

5. **Professional advice is not optional** for significant pension decisions – it's essential and, in some cases (like DB transfers over £30,000), legally required.

6. **This appendix is for understanding concepts** so you can have more informed conversations with professional advisers – it is not a substitute for that advice.

Always consult FCA-regulated, qualified pension advisers before making pension decisions.

Appendix C: Tax Planning – Educational Framework

CRITICAL TAX DISCLAIMER: Tax law in the UK is extremely complex, changes frequently, and applies differently based on individual circumstances. This appendix provides only a very high-level educational overview of certain tax concepts that exist within UK legislation.

This is not tax advice. Tax planning decisions should always be based on professional advice specific to your complete circumstances. Incorrect tax planning can result in:

- Unexpected tax bills and interest charges
- HMRC penalties for incorrect returns
- Anti-avoidance provisions being applied
- Loss of expected tax benefits

The rates and allowances mentioned reflect the 2024/25 tax year as understood at the time of writing. Tax legislation changes regularly, and allowances are often adjusted annually. Always verify current tax rules before any decision.

Furthermore, this appendix contains only a summary of complex rules. Professional tax advice is essential before implementing any tax planning. If you're unsure about terminology or whether any of these concepts apply to you, consult a qualified tax adviser or accountant.

C1: ISA Planning Principles

ISAs are tax-advantaged savings and investment accounts available in the UK. This section provides educational information about how they work.

ISA Annual Subscription Limit

Current rules (2024/25 tax year):

- Annual subscription limit: £20,000 across all ISA types
- Can split between Cash ISA and Stocks & Shares ISA within the overall limit
- Junior ISAs have separate limit (£9,000 for 2024/25)
- Use-it-or-lose-it: unused allowance doesn't carry forward

Tax Treatment of ISAs

Money held in ISAs receives preferential tax treatment:

- No income tax on interest or dividends earned within ISA
- No capital gains tax on growth within ISA
- Withdrawals are tax-free
- ISAs form part of your estate for inheritance tax purposes

Common ISA Planning Considerations Discussed

Financial commentary often discusses various ISA planning concepts:

Asset location considerations:

- Some commentators suggest prioritising assets with highest growth potential in tax-free wrappers
- Tax efficiency varies based on individual tax position
- What's efficient for one person may not be for another

Timing considerations:

- Contributing earlier in the tax year provides longer tax-free growth period
- Must balance against other financial priorities and cash flow
- No benefit to waiting if funds are available

Cash vs Stocks & Shares ISA considerations:

- Emergency funds might be held in Cash ISAs for accessibility
- Longer-term goals might use Stocks & Shares ISAs for growth potential
- Interest rate environment affects relative attractiveness of cash
- Individual risk tolerance matters significantly

ISA vs Pension – Key Differences

These are fundamentally different products with different features and tax treatment:

Feature	ISA	Pension
Tax relief on contributions	No	Yes (20–45%)
Tax on growth	Tax-free	Tax-free
Access	Any time	Age 55+ (rising to 57 in 2028)
Annual limit	£20,000	£60,000 (or 100% earnings)
Inheritance tax	Part of estate	Usually outside estate
Flexibility	Complete	Limited before pension age

Factors to consider when comparing ISA vs pension contributions:

- Your current marginal tax rate vs expected retirement rate
- When you need access to the money
- Inheritance planning considerations
- Overall tax position and other income sources
- Whether you've maximised employer pension matching

Common observations in financial planning commentary:

- Higher rate taxpayers receive 40% tax relief on pension contributions (significant immediate benefit)
- Basic rate taxpayers receive 20% relief (more modest benefit)
- ISAs provide complete access flexibility
- Pensions have inheritance tax advantages

These are general observations about the products, not recommendations for your situation. The right answer depends on comprehensive financial planning.

Lifetime ISA (LISA) – Key Features

The Lifetime ISA is a specific ISA type with different rules:

Key features:

- Annual contribution limit: £4,000 (within overall £20,000 ISA allowance)
- Government bonus: 25% on contributions (maximum £1,000 annually)
- Age restrictions: Must be 18–39 to open; can contribute until age 50
- Usage restrictions: Can only be withdrawn without penalty for first home purchase (up to £450,000) or after age 60
- Withdrawal penalty: 25% charge on withdrawals for other purposes (loses bonus plus some capital)

Common LISA considerations:

- Can be useful for first-time buyers getting government bonus
- Can supplement retirement savings with government top-up
- Withdrawal penalty is significant deterrent for other uses
- Must be sure you won't need money for other purposes before 60

Important limitations:

- Penalty on withdrawal can exceed the bonus received
- Property price limit may exclude some areas
- Counts toward overall ISA allowance
- Complex rules around first home purchases

C2: Capital Gains Tax (CGT) – Basic Concepts

Capital Gains Tax applies to profits when selling certain assets. This section provides educational overview.

Annual Exempt Amount

Current rule (2024/25): £3,000

- Each individual has an annual CGT allowance
- Gains below this threshold aren't taxed
- Allowance can't be carried forward if unused
- Married couples/civil partners each have their own allowance

CGT Rates (2024/25)

Tax rates depend on your total taxable income and the type of asset:

For most assets:

- Basic rate taxpayers: 10% (18% for residential property)
- Higher/additional rate taxpayers: 20% (24% for residential property)

TAX-LOSS HARVESTING – CONCEPT OVERVIEW

"Tax-loss harvesting" refers to the practice of realising investment losses to offset gains for tax purposes. Key concepts:

How it works in principle:

- Investment losses can offset gains in the same tax year
- Excess losses can be carried forward to future years
- Net gains after losses are compared to annual exempt amount

The "30-day rule":

- HMRC has rules to prevent "wash sales" (selling and immediately repurchasing to create artificial losses)
- If you repurchase the same or substantially similar asset within 30 days, the loss may not be allowable
- Rules are complex and specific

Important considerations:

- Transaction costs may outweigh tax benefits
- Market timing risk if waiting 30 days to repurchase
- Record-keeping requirements are significant
- Rules around "same or substantially similar" assets are complex

Spousal transfer considerations:

- Assets can be transferred between spouses/civil partners without triggering CGT
- Each spouse has their own annual exempt amount
- Can potentially utilise both allowances
- Requires proper planning and record-keeping

This is a complex area where professional tax advice is valuable.

- "Bed and ISA" Arrangements – Educational Overview
- "Bed and ISA" refers to selling investments and repurchasing them within an ISA wrapper. Conceptually:

How it works:

- Sell investments in a general investment account
- Realise any capital gain (ideally within annual exempt amount)
- Immediately repurchase same investments inside ISA wrapper
- Future growth is then tax-free within ISA

Theoretical benefits:

- Moves assets into tax-free wrapper
- Can utilise annual CGT allowance
- Can utilise annual ISA allowance
- Future gains sheltered from CGT

Important considerations and risks:

- Market movement risk during the transaction
- Transaction costs
- Must have available ISA allowance
- Potential breach of 30-day rule if not structured correctly (though different rules may apply)
- Some platforms offer this as a specific service

This technique requires careful implementation and professional advice to ensure compliance with tax rules.

C3: Inheritance Tax (IHT) – Overview of Concepts

Inheritance Tax is charged on estates above certain thresholds. This is an extremely complex area of tax law.

IHT Thresholds (2024/25)

Nil Rate Band: £325,000

- First £325,000 of estate is usually tax-free
- Unused nil rate band can transfer to surviving spouse/civil partner (potentially doubling to £650,000)

Residence Nil Rate Band: £175,000

- Additional allowance when passing main residence to direct descendants
- Tapers away for estates over £2 million
- Can also transfer to surviving spouse (potentially £350,000 total)
- Complex qualifying conditions apply

IHT Rate: 40% on estate above available allowances

Spouse/Civil Partner Exemption: Unlimited transfers between spouses during life or on death (if both UK-domiciled)

Gifting Rules – Overview

UK tax law contains various exemptions and reliefs for lifetime gifts:

Annual Exemptions:

- £3,000 annual gift exemption per person
- Can carry forward one year if unused
- Small gifts exemption: £250 per recipient per year (separate from £3,000)
- Wedding/civil partnership gifts: Varies by relationship (£5,000 to children, £2,500 to grandchildren, £1,000 to others)

Regular Gifts from Income:

- Gifts made regularly from surplus income may be immediately exempt
- Must be able to demonstrate pattern and that gifts don't reduce standard of living
- Requires detailed record-keeping
- HMRC may scrutinise these claims

Potentially Exempt Transfers (PETs)

Gifts above the exemptions may become "Potentially Exempt Transfers":

Key concepts:

- Gift is immediately out of estate for IHT if donor survives 7 years
- If donor dies within 7 years, gift may be taxable
- Taper relief reduces tax (not the value) after 3 years
- Complex rules about who pays any tax due

Taper relief on tax (not on value):

- Years 0–3: Full tax if applicable
- Years 3–4: 80% of tax charged
- Years 4–5: 60% of tax charged
- Years 5–6: 40% of tax charged
- Years 6–7: 20% of tax charged
- After 7 years: No tax

Critical misunderstandings to avoid:

- Taper relief reduces the tax, not the value of the gift
- Gifts may still affect the nil rate band available for the estate
- Complex rules about order of gifts and who pays tax
- Record-keeping is essential
- Charitable Giving and IHT
- Gifts to qualifying charities have special tax treatment

Key features:

- Gifts to charity are fully exempt from IHT (during life and in will)
- If 10% or more of net estate is left to charity, IHT rate reduces from 40% to 36%
- Complex calculation to determine whether 10% threshold is met

Important considerations:

- Whether the 36% rate saves tax depends on estate size and circumstances
- Calculation is based on "baseline amount" which is complex
- May not be beneficial for smaller estates
- Other factors beyond tax should influence charitable giving decisions
- IHT Planning – Critical Warnings

Inheritance tax planning is one of the most complex areas of personal taxation:

- Rules interact with domicile, residence, and international issues
- Anti-avoidance provisions apply to many planning techniques
- "Gifts with reservation of benefit" can fail entirely
- Trust planning has its own complex tax regime
- Changes in circumstances can undermine planning
- Timing of gifts matters significantly

Common IHT planning mistakes:

- Making gifts but retaining benefit (e.g., gifting house but continuing to live there rent-free)
- Not keeping adequate records of gifts and exemptions
- Assuming life insurance solves all problems
- Over-simplifying complex family situations
- Not coordinating IHT planning with overall financial planning

Professional advice from specialists in IHT planning is essential. This is not an area for DIY planning beyond the most straightforward gifting exemptions.

C4: Income Tax – Overview of Allowances

This section provides overview of income tax allowances that may be relevant to investment income.

Key Allowances (2024/25)

Personal Allowance: £12,570

- Tax-free income allowance for most people
- Reduces by £1 for every £2 earned over £100,000
- Completely withdrawn at £125,140

Dividend Allowance: £500

- First £500 of dividend income tax-free (after personal allowance)
- Dividends above this taxed at: 8.75% (basic), 33.75% (higher), 39.35% (additional rate)

Personal Savings Allowance:

- Basic rate taxpayers: £1,000 of savings interest tax-free
- Higher rate taxpayers: £500 of savings interest tax-free
- Additional rate taxpayers: £0 (no allowance)

Starting Rate for Savings: £5,000 at 0%

- Only available if total taxable income (excluding savings) is below personal allowance
- Complex interaction with other income
- Rarely applicable for higher earners
- Income Tax Planning Considerations
- Financial planning commentary often discusses various considerations for managing taxable income:

Using allowances efficiently:

- Utilising dividend and savings allowances before they're taxed
- ISA wrapper eliminates tax on investment income entirely
- Pension contributions reduce taxable income and create tax relief

Marginal rate management:

- Those near tax thresholds (£50,270 for higher rate, £100,000 for personal allowance withdrawal) may benefit from reviewing income timing
- Pension contributions reduce "adjusted income" for threshold purposes
- Charitable donations under Gift Aid extend basic rate band

Asset location considerations:

- Income-generating assets might be more tax-efficient in ISAs
- Capital growth assets might be more suitable for GIAs if within CGT allowance
- Individual circumstances vary significantly

Illustrative Income Tax Example

This example illustrates concepts only and should not be used for decision-making:

Hypothetical scenario: Someone earning £55,000 (£5,000 above higher rate threshold) considering £5,000 pension contribution:

Without pension contribution:

- £5,000 taxed at 40% higher rate = £2,000 tax
- Plus 2% National Insurance on income over £50,270 = £100
- Total tax on this £5,000: £2,100

With pension contribution:

- Adjusted income: £50,000 (now within basic rate band)
- Tax saved: £2,100
- Plus receives basic rate tax relief on pension: 20% × £5,000 = £1,000
- Total higher rate relief: £2,000 (difference between 40% and 20%)

Important caveats:

- This is simplified and assumes specific circumstances
- Doesn't consider other factors like student loans, child benefit charge, etc.
- Tax relief mechanisms work differently for different pension arrangements
- Individual circumstances vary
- This is not advice to make pension contributions

C5: Tax Considerations in Retirement – Educational Overview

How you withdraw money in retirement has tax implications. This section discusses concepts commonly considered.

Sources of Retirement Income – Tax Treatment

Different sources of retirement income have different tax treatments:

State Pension:

- Taxable as earned income
- No tax deducted at source (paid gross)
- Uses up personal allowance

Private Pensions:

- Usually 25% available as tax-free lump sum
- Remaining 75% taxed as income when withdrawn
- Can take tax-free element gradually or as lump sum

ISA Withdrawals:

- Completely tax-free
- Don't count toward taxable income
- Don't affect personal allowance

General Investment Accounts:

- Dividends subject to dividend tax (after £500 allowance)
- Interest subject to income tax (after personal savings allowance if available)
- Capital gains subject to CGT when investments sold

Other Sources:

- Rental income taxable (after allowable expenses)
- Employment/self-employment income taxable as normal

Withdrawal Sequencing – Common Considerations

Financial planning often discusses the order in which to draw down different assets in retirement. Common considerations include:

Tax efficiency considerations:

- Using personal allowance efficiently
- Managing marginal tax rates
- Utilising allowances (dividend, savings, CGT)
- Coordinating different income sources

Factors affecting withdrawal order:

- Current and projected tax rates
- Required minimum withdrawals (if applicable)
- Investment time horizons
- Estate planning objectives
- Liquidity needs
- Market conditions

Commonly discussed approaches:

- Drawing from taxable accounts first to let tax-advantaged accounts grow
- Alternatively, using tax-free sources (ISAs, pension tax-free cash) early
- Taking pension income up to personal allowance then supplementing from ISAs
- Coordinating State Pension commencement with private pension withdrawals

Illustrative Withdrawal Example
This example illustrates concepts only:

Hypothetical scenario: Someone needs £30,000 annual income in retirement with State Pension of £11,500:

Approach 1: All from pension

- State Pension: £11,500 (uses personal allowance)
- Need additional: £18,500 from private pension
- Tax on £18,500 at basic rate (assuming within £50,270): £3,700
- Net after tax: £26,300 available from £30,000 income

Approach 2: Mixed sources

- State Pension: £11,500 (uses personal allowance)
- Private pension: £5,000 (keeps total at £16,500, still within personal allowance due to other factors)
- ISA withdrawal: £13,500 (tax-free)
- Total tax: Potentially minimal to zero depending on full circumstances

Critical disclaimers:

- This is highly simplified and hypothetical
- Actual tax calculation depends on complete circumstances
- Doesn't consider NI credits, marriage allowance, or other factors
- State Pension amount varies by individual NI record
- May be other income sources to consider
- This is not advice about how you should structure withdrawals

Retirement income planning is complex and requires professional financial planning advice tailored to your complete circumstances.

References & Further Reading for Financial Confidence

Every idea in Smart Money, Strong Women has been shaped by research, lived experience, and the work of many pioneering women and thinkers who've helped redefine money, confidence, and freedom.

Here you'll find the key studies, reports, and resources that informed this book – alongside books, podcasts, and communities to help you continue your own financial journey with confidence and curiosity.

Core Research & References

Bank of England (2023). *Financial Lives Survey.* **www.bankofengland.co.uk**

Barclays (2022). *The Financial Wellbeing Index.* **www.barclays.co.uk**

Behavioural Insights Team (2021). *Improving Women's Financial Resilience.* **www.bi.team**

Department for Work and Pensions (DWP) (2024). *Pensions Policy Statement: Gender Disparities in Retirement Outcomes.* **www.gov.uk/dwp**

Department for Work and Pensions (DWP) (2024). *Gender Pensions Gap in Private Pensions: 2020 to 2022.* **www.gov.uk/government/organisations/department-for-work-and-pensions**

FCA (2023). *Financial Lives: Women and Financial Vulnerability.* **www.fca.org.uk/publications**

Fawcett Society (2022). *Menopause and the Workplace.* **www.fawcettsociety.org.uk**

Fidelity International (2022). *The Financial Power of Women: Closing the Gender Investment Gap.* **www.fidelity.co.uk**

Institute for Fiscal Studies (IFS) (2023). *Gender Pay and Pension Gaps in the UK.* **www.ifs.org.uk**

Legal & General (2023). *Divorce and Finances Research Findings.* **www.legalandgeneral.com**

McKinsey & Company (2023). *Women in the Workplace Report.* **www.mckinsey.com/women-in-the-workplace**

Money and Pensions Service (MaPS) (2023). *Financial Wellbeing Survey: UK Findings.* **www.moneyandpensionsservice.org.uk**

Office for National Statistics (ONS) (2020). *Human Capital Estimates in the UK: 2004 to 2018.* **www.ons.gov.uk**

Office for National Statistics (ONS) (2023). *The Impact of Motherhood on Monthly Employee Earnings and Employment Status (England), 2014 to 2022.* **www.ons.gov.uk**

Office for National Statistics (ONS) (2024). *Gender Pay Gap in the UK: 2024.* www.ons.gov.uk

OECD (2022). *Gender and Financial Literacy: Evidence from the OECD/INFE Survey.* www.oecd.org/finance/financial-education

Trades Union Congress (TUC) (2025). *Gender Pensions Gap Report.* www.tuc.org.uk

UBS (2023). *Own Your Worth: The Financial Participation Gap Between Men and Women.* www.ubs.com/women

Women's Budget Group (2023). *Gender and Wealth in the UK.* www.wbg.org.uk

World Economic Forum (2023). *Global Gender Gap Report.* www.weforum.org/reports/global-gender-gap-report

Further Reading & Resources for Financial Confidence

Money Mindset & Behaviour

Housel, M. (2020). *The Psychology of Money.* London: Harriman House.
→ A timeless exploration of how emotion, ego and identity drive financial decisions far more than logic.

Lowry, Clare Seal (2023). *Five Steps to Financial Wellbeing.*
→ Practical, compassionate guidance for managing money anxiety and building confidence.

Scarlett, Selina (2021). *Money Lessons: How to Manage Your Finances to Get the Life You Want.*
→ Realistic, accessible advice for women at all life stages.

Women, Work & Wealth

Criado Perez, C. (2019). *Invisible Women: Exposing Data Bias in a World Designed for Men.*
→ A must-read to understand how gendered systems shape economics, careers, and finance.

Sethi, R. (2020). *I Will Teach You to Be Rich* (Updated Edition).
→ Modern, witty, and full of practical tools – particularly empowering for women starting to invest.

Fidelity Women & Money Study. [Online].
Available at: www.fidelity.co.uk/learning/women-and-money
→ Regularly updated research into women's investment habits, confidence gaps and financial goals.

Investing & Financial Independence

FIRE UK Community. www.reddit.com/r/UKPersonalFinance
→ Community-led advice and accountability for those seeking financial independence and early retirement.

Khalifa, Bola Sol (2022). *How to Save It: Fix Your Finances.*
→ Candid, relatable, and inclusive – particularly good for readers starting from scratch.

Morgan Stanley (2023). *Women, Wealth, and Investing Report.* [Online]. Available at: www.morganstanley.com/articles/women-wealth

Podcasts & Audio Learning

BBC Money Box. Weekly insight into financial news, policy changes, and consumer issues. www.bbc.co.uk/programmes/b006qps9

The Meaningful Money Podcast (Pete Matthew). Practical steps and jargon-free investing education. www.meaningfulmoney.tv

She Makes Money Moves (Refinery29). Real women, real money stories. www.refinery29.com/en-gb/she-makes-money-moves-podcast

Financial Feminist (Tori Dunlap). Global community focused on closing the financial confidence gap. www.herfirst100k.com/financial-feminist-podcast

Supportive Organisations & Learning Platforms

MoneyHelper (MaPS). Free, impartial money and pension guidance. www.moneyhelper.org.uk

StepChange Debt Charity. Confidential debt advice and support. www.stepchange.org

Women's Budget Group. Research and advocacy for economic equality. www.wbg.org.uk

MyWealthVault. Eva Wealth's financial platform for women of all ages and stages of their wealth journey. www.mywealthvault.co.uk

Eva Wealth. Expert financial guidance and education for women navigating change. www.evawealth.co.uk

Closing Note

Each of these sources offers another step forward on your journey:
to deepen your knowledge, question what you've been told, and shape a financial life that feels authentic, confident, and free.

Keep reading, keep asking, and keep rebelling with purpose.

About the Author

Sarah Roughsedge is a chartered financial planner and financial coach with a background in neuroscience. As the award-winning founder of Eva Wealth, she's dedicated to transforming the way women experience money, blending mindset change with a firm belief that empowerment begins long before the spreadsheets. Her work has been featured in the Financial Times and on BBC Woman's Hour, where she champions clarity, confidence, and financial empowerment without jargon or judgement.

---

www.instagram.com/evawealthforwomen

www.linkedin.com/in/sarahroughsedge

www.evawealth.co.uk

Made in the USA
Monee, IL
04 November 2026

67383149R10146